C000129652

UNLOCKING THE WORLD'S LARGEST E-MARKET

A GUIDE TO SELLING ON CHINESE SOCIAL MEDIA

Rave Reviews

"Ashley is the go-to guru for Chinese social media. This book distills a lot of her expertise and should be kept on your desk."
-- Jeffrey Towson, Managing Partner, Towson Capital

"Ashley Galina Dudarenok has written a clear, analytical guide to digital marketing on Chinese social media. Merely projecting Western e-marketing onto the Chinese markets and platforms is unlikely to work; Dudarenok explains in readable detail why not and what to do about it."
-- Peter Gordon, Editor of Asian Review of Books

"Ashley's book provides a view of the current situation, some really good insights into what's coming down the line and some very practical tips and steps. It's a must-read for any marketer and business owner who is planning to enter China, or is operating in the China market already."
--Martin Newman, Executive Chairman of Practicology

"In this fresh-eyed, easy to understand book, Ms. Dudarenok deftly explains the intersection of e-commerce, technology and social media as the key drivers of "The New Retail" in China and the ways in which Chinese e-commerce and technology companies are influencing and changing global technology."
-- Michael Zakkour, VP Tompkins International, China/APAC & Global E-commerce Practices, author of China's Super Consumers

"With the convergence of consumerism, social media and mobile payments in China, the time is right for this book. Dudarenok gives both nuanced insights and practical recommendations for companies seeking success in penetrating this complex market."
-- Fredda McDonald, Managing Director of World 50 Inc.

"This step-by-step guide quickly takes you from a 10,000-foot view to on the ground tactics, providing a roadmap for navigating China's complexity and ensuring the ability to capitalize on this bourgeoning market."
-- R. Danielle Bailey, Head of APAC Research at L2 Inc.

"Ashley's book, the most exhaustive piece of work done about WeChat to date, is essential for marketers and innovators or anyone who wants to be a true WeChat expert."
-- Thomas Meyer, Co-founder of Mobile Now Group

"China means 1.4 billion potential customers. Every fourth person is in the middle class and it will probably be every second person very soon. You can't overlook China anymore."
-- Jan Smejkal, China & APAC Community Director at Startup Grind

"Ashley does a remarkable job at giving a comprehensive and insightful picture of the modern Chinese digital landscape. Whether you're just discovering the Chinese Internet or want to deepen your understanding, Ashley's work is a must-read."
-- Thomas Graziani, Co-founder of WalktheChat

"Ashley has done an excellent job of boiling down the extremely complex world of Chinese marketing, giving readers a concise overview without any of the fluff! The book provides a ton of useful information both at a macro and micro level."
-- Lauren Hallanan, Host of the China Influencer Marketing Podcast

"Ashley brings you all you need to know about Chinese social media. It's a comprehensive book giving you a complete and practical overview of the market so you can start marketing in China as soon as possible."
-- Shlomo Freund, Founder of Free Financial Self and AppInChina

*To all those crazy marketers
who decided to take their brand to China.
This book is for you.*

CONTENTS

PART I

What Every Marketer Needs to Know about China

CHAPTER 1

Why You Need to Be in the China Market

With more than 1.3 billion people, China still tops the board with the world's largest population. It also has the world's largest e-commerce economy, which was worth 7.57 trillion RMB (1.18 trillion USD) in 2017.

It's a huge market full of potential but it's not straightforward. Before stepping into this unique market, there are five things you must know in advance.

China is not a single market

In this book, "the China market" is used as shorthand for speed and clarity but the truth is China is not one market. Different groups and regions have different needs and experience different trends. It's actually a collection of 34 distinct markets, which correspond to China's administrative divisions.

Think about it. You'd never sell to someone in Iceland the same way you'd sell to someone in Italy. And you'd never sell to someone in rural Arkansas the way you'd sell to someone in Los Angeles. They're different.

The same principle applies in China and that's what makes it a much more complicated market than people realize. There are no one-size-fits-all situations or solutions when one talks about China.

In this book, broad trends and market forces are outlined. Most apply to 1st and 2nd tier cities and the middle class throughout the country but you must do research for your industry, your product, the region you are entering and so on before entering the market.

There are 2 uniting forces

Mandarin

Mandarin, also known as Putonghua, is the national language which was adopted nationwide in 1932. Its pronunciation is based on the Beijing dialect and it's written using simplified Chinese characters. Whether you're in Urumqi, Harbin or Guangzhou, people speak Mandarin in addition to any local dialect.

Social Media Mania

Every day, Chinese people log in to their social media accounts to receive the latest news, connect with friends and family and contact brands and vendors to make enquiries, complaints and purchases.

They also browse on a variety of online sales channels, including Taobao, Tmall and JD.com to find the latest products and sales campaigns. Convenient mobile payment apps, like Alipay and WeChat Pay, and express delivery services facilitate their online purchases.

Nearly everyone in China is not just on social media but active on it. In the early days of social media, it was very attractive to people because it was one of the few places you could talk to people in different parts of China and the world anonymously. It was a hotline to the latest news that was hard to find elsewhere. Over time, it became an accepted part of daily life.

In the West, when social media began to take hold, users could connect with friends using Facebook, search for information and news using Google and then go to a big box store like Walmart or log onto Amazon to buy things easily and cheaply.

In China, several steps in the Western path were skipped or shortened. Platforms like QQ, WeChat and Weibo retained users by making their services more efficient and expansive which made the average person's life easier. Sites and apps included as many functions as possible and offered increasingly personalized features to keep users within their platform. For mobile users, features were designed to keep their phone memory and data usage low.

They also catered specifically to local culture and customs. Features like red packets (red envelopes with money in them) for Chinese New Year and as quick gifts or payments to friends took off. The voice message feature is also widely used so people can avoid the extra time it takes to type complicated Chinese characters. Platforms are constantly testing new features that can improve the experience of Chinese users. It's made life a lot easier for people and fits in perfectly with the rise of the mobile internet.

The market is oversupplied

Since the economic reforms of the late 1970s, international brands have been trying to sell their products to Chinese consumers. Together with local brands, they offer a wide array of products for consumers to choose from.

This broad selection of outstanding products has made Chinese consumers increasingly picky. It's also created a rather fragmented market and has produced fierce competition between brands making it hard for newcomers. This means brands that have not already entered the market need to do thorough research into the status for their industry and product category to see if the market could really be profitable before taking the next step.

Shopping is a national strategy in China

Private consumption in China has grown at a rapid pace in the past decade and retail sales have grown at double-digit rates for years. It's now the primary driver of China's economic growth.

China's economic growth used to depend heavily on exports. However, with a growing internal economy, improved economic infrastructure, a slump in international market demand, appreciation of the yuan and increasing labour costs, the importance of exports has decreased in recent years. Its transition to a more sustainable mode is driven by consumption, the service industry and innovation.

This is why China has been encouraging people to shop more to stimulate domestic demand and boost consumption-driven growth.

Social media marketing and mobile payments are king

Chinese consumers are moving from brick-and-mortar stores to online channels. They not only flock to major e-commerce platforms but are also leveraging all kinds of social media platforms to look for product information, get recommendations from bloggers and peers, seek out customer service and even purchase directly.

China's social media mania unites consumer groups with diverse purchasing behaviours in a large, fragmented market. This means a prominent presence on social media is an entry point for newcomers and essential for those already in the market.

With more and more people shopping online and the rapid development of mobile tech and networks, the popularity of mobile payments in China is increasing and Chinese people are using less and less cash. And mobile payment apps are not just used online. Smartphones and tablets are everywhere in China and payments through apps are widely accepted in brick-and-mortar stores. The country is developing a cashless retail ecosystem, although there will still be a role for cash for the foreseeable future. To achieve success in China, full compatibility with China's mobile payment systems and China's overall e-commerce ecosystem is vital.

Whether you're an entrepreneur who plans to do business in China or not, you need to know about these developments if you want to stay ahead of the game. Although these transformations are currently taking place in China, their effects will be felt elsewhere and will travel beyond its borders. Social media is not an option in this market. It's a requirement.

CHAPTER 2

What You Need to Know About Chinese Consumers

Understanding the mindset and preferences of Chinese consumers is the key to the China market. To understand these things, one must first understand the path they've taken in the past 30-40 years. Then the different kinds of consumers in China now and the types of consumers that are emerging in the fastest changing market in the world can be examined. It's a vast nation with lots of trends and regional diversity but the integration of social media in daily life and increasing purchasing power are affecting the whole country.

2.1 The Development of Modern Chinese Consumers

Consumer behaviour in China started to change and evolve in the late 1970s after reforms and the opening-up policy were adopted. The path can be divided into several phases.

In the 1980s

In this decade, right after the initiation of key reform policies, the growth of the domestic economy resulted in a continuous rise in incomes and consumption levels. In the mid-1980s, a limited number of international goods made their way into China and a market-based system was formed to replace the planned economy. At first, Chinese consumers could only purchase international goods from a few designated state-owned stores. As time went on, rules were relaxed little by little. Chinese companies could set up privately-owned entities to sell both domestic and foreign goods. Then foreign companies were allowed to set up joint ventures to retail products in brick-and-mortar stores or through other sales channels. Finally, foreign retailers and brands could operate on their own in China.

With more money at their disposal, Chinese consumers' thirst for consumption grew quickly, especially for daily necessities. Another benefit of economic reform was that Chinese people finally had an opportunity to learn more about other countries. They envied the good living conditions and high living standards in foreign countries. It was during this time that they started to cultivate a preference for international brands and imported goods. Things were just getting started.

In the 1990s

China then progressed to being a sellers' market. With limited access to information, consumers tended to show conformity when purchasing and often "followed the crowd". If they saw someone with a special item, then they wanted one too. For those with the means, there wasn't much thought about need or practicality. This was a phase of buying what you saw, instead of thinking critically.

During this time, awareness of the concept of "consumers" gradually emerged. However, consumer credit remained an unknown field.

After 2000

From 2000-2010, Chinese consumers matured as more and more products became available to them. The whole market slowly transformed into a buyers' market.

During this period, they showed more thought when selecting products. As there were more and more goods to choose from, they started to compare them in price and quality before buying. At the same time, concerns over product quality and safety were raised.

Unlike the previous decade, they began to abandon the habit of following the crowd. Instead, they wanted to show their personality and distinguish themselves with their purchases. Frequent shifts in interests, styles and personalities were reflected in the way they selected products. They were willing to try different styles and types of products to show "they were what they bought". They started to have more requests. As their tastes changed frequently, brands and merchants needed to respond quickly to fast-moving trends in order to succeed.

2.2 Today's Consumers

While the majority of Chinese consumers are not in the affluent or middle-income groups, there's a huge middle class and it's growing. This book focuses on this increasing segment of the population.

People in their late 20s and early 30s who live in urban areas are part of this growing middle class. They're generally better educated than their parents and tend to save less despite the fact that they earn sizable incomes. Although China's economic growth has been slowing down in the past few years, these consumers are optimistic that their earnings and living standards will increase and improve over time. They not only buy things for themselves but also for their family. They often shop online but they prioritize value and quality over low prices.

In the past, practicality and price were the factors Chinese consumers cared about most. Now they're becoming more sophisticated and trading up from mass market to stylish, premium products. Now that the market is saturated with both international and local brands, consumers have higher expectations and can be pickier. This is one of the reasons why recommendations on social media have become more powerful than traditional advertising.

China has more than 700 million monthly active users on social media and 300 million consumers shopping online. It's become a trend for some and a lifestyle for others and, taken all together, it makes for fantastic sales potential for brands. China is the world's largest e-commerce economy with a wide range of online shopping options. Platforms such as Taobao, Tmall, JD.com and Xiaohongshu are highly integrated with social media, mobile payment apps and delivery services.

While e-commerce has taken off, traditional shopping and marketing haven't died. Shopping in malls and standalone stores is still popular and many Chinese people even go abroad to buy luxury goods in person. Shopping tourism is a growing trend in China.

Understanding this rapidly evolving target audience is essential, on and off line. Let's take a closer look.

City Tiers

In the 1980s, the Chinese government introduced a ranking system to facilitate a staged rollout of infrastructure and urban development. At first, cities were ranked by tier according to the government's development priorities. Later, with the growing economy, this ranking started to take more criteria into consideration, including population, economic size and political ranking. The rankings change from time to time depending on how the ratings are done but there's broad general agreement on them.

China's first tier cities are four of the largest and wealthiest. They are key political, commercial or industrial centres – Beijing, Shanghai, Guangzhou and Shenzhen. Second tier cities are mainly provincial capitals and coastal cities, like Chengdu, Wuhan and Xiamen. Third tier cities are medium-sized cities in each province, while other smaller cities are grouped into fourth tier cities.

Most consumption comes from first and second tier cities and other urban areas with high per capita income. As for e-commerce consumption, second and third tier cities account for an increasing portion of online spending. People in Beijing and Shanghai, have a disposable personal income (DPI) level of more than 52,000 RMB/year (around 8,200 USD) while Tianjin and Shenzhen closely follow behind with more than 38,000 RMB/year (around 6,000 USD) DPI.

Although consumers from second tier cities earn nearly as much as those in first tier cities, they have fewer options for shopping so they tend to purchase online to fill this gap. Also, compared to first tier cities, consumers from second tier cities have more free time to do online shopping meaning greater opportunities for online retailers in these markets.

China continues to rapidly urbanize. It's estimated that 60% of the population will live in urban areas by 2020. This means 100 million more people will become urban consumers and McKinsey predicts that the per capita disposable income of these consumers will double between 2010 and 2020 from about 4,000 USD to 8,000 USD.

Age Groups

China's main consumer force is made up of people between 17 and 36 years old. They're the post-80s and post-90s generations who make up the majority of online consumers.

Most of them are university students, fresh graduates, newcomers to the workforce and young parents. They not only buy things for themselves, but also for their parents and children. They're generally better educated, tend to save less, spend more on entertainment than their parents and often shop online. They prioritize value and quality over low prices.

At the same time, it's worth noting that consumers above 60 years of age also make up 11.2% of online consumers. They have more money and time at their disposal after retirement and are a growing segment of the population.

Sophisticated and Spoiled

There's a stereotype of Chinese consumers as behind-the-times bargain hunters. People think of the "organized tour tourists": everyone following the group flag-bearer, wearing matching caps and going from souvenir shop to souvenir shop. These consumers exist but many young city dwellers have moved beyond these clichés.

Chinese consumers are the most sophisticated and spoiled consumers in the world. Why?

1.   The market is flooded. There's an oversupply of products to choose from. Ever since economic reforms took hold in the 1970s, international brands have been entering the market, eager to reach 1.3 billion potential customers. Together with local brands, they offer a wide range of products for consumers to choose from. People with higher incomes can select the most outstanding products while those of more modest means still have great choice.

2.   People now ask for and expect high quality, personalized customer service. Many seem to believe that not only is the customer always right but that the customer is God. Therefore, they pay great attention to a brand's customer service.

With the popularity of social media, Chinese consumers constantly use it to contact brands with enquiries and complaints. Although digital channels offer rapid, straightforward "non-human" assistance, Chinese consumers still prefer a real person to solve their customer service issues.

Most Chinese consumers prefer human interaction when they need assistance and 79% are willing to pay more if it ensures a better level of customer service. For those with unsatisfactory customer service, 27% said they would never go back to them again.

Given these high expectations, brands work hard to provide their best service and cater to customers not only inside China, but also abroad, when these customers travel. Over 62 million Chinese citizens travelled abroad during the first half of 2017 and many expect these numbers to increase in the coming decade.

3. Chinese consumers are used to a variety of convenient options when it comes to shopping. Mobile payments are ubiquitous. Buying items featured in a livestream while it's streaming is not unusual and making purchases through social media is also normal. They expect brands and platforms to streamline commercial processes for the customer's ease.

Having experienced such convenience and high-quality customer service, Chinese consumers now have higher expectations of brands. To please these picky consumers, brands need to step up their game.

2.3 Emerging Consumer Groups

Chinese consumers are changing all the time. So are consumer groups. Here we've picked some emerging consumer groups that are important for brands to take note of due to their growing influence.

Seniors

China is an aging society with relatively high life expectancy and low birth rate. With higher living standards and advanced medical services, the average life expectancy in China is 75.7 years. Those same higher living standards led to a reduction in birth rates and the government has now moved from a one-child policy, introduced in the late 1970s, to a policy allowing two children in some circumstances. The average birth rate in China in 2016 was 12.95 births per 1,000 people while the global average was 18.5 births per 1,000.

As a result, China is facing the problem of an aging population. Some estimates show that by the year 2050, the number of Chinese citizens over the age of 65 is expected to reach 329 million. The growing population of senior citizens in China makes it an emerging consumer group in the foreseeable future.

Instead of staying at home and looking after their grandchildren, modern seniors are more willing to pursue a lavish lifestyle than previous generations. They're cultivating their own interests and travelling. About 20% of Chinese travellers in 2015 were 60 or above. This presents huge potential for offerings such as travel packages designed for senior citizens.

Health products and medical services are also in strong demand for this group. However, it's also worth noting that demand for maternity and baby products is also expected to grow as people expect the birth rate to rise gradually in the coming years.

Single Young People

Economic growth in China has also driven development in education. Children are told from a young age that they need to study hard to get a well-paying job and make a good living. Since the late 1970s, education levels in China have continued improving. The number of tertiary graduates per year has increased from 1,775,999 in 2000 to 11,923,653 in 2015.

Young people in China, are increasingly postponing marriage and childbearing. Some are aiming for higher education levels, career advancement and higher social status while others think it costs too much to get married. They're more willing to stay single and spend money on themselves. By some estimates, the number of single adults in China has reached 200 million, equivalent to the combined populations of Russia and the United Kingdom.

Since they don't need to take care of a family yet, they spend more time and money on entertainment and recreation with friends or colleagues. This has boosted the importance of the "singles' economy". For example, they may go to a restaurant, the cinema or karaoke (KTV) alone. Places that offer solo seats and that let them be part of the crowd without standing out will be their first choice. Smaller apartments and tiny appliances for solo living are also popular with this group. During the 2017 11.11 Shopping Festival*, purchases of mini-appliances rose 92% and "one-person use" sales were up 190%. In a related trend, sales of pet-related items and accessories were up 239% as single people sought companionship.

* Singles' Day on Nov. 11th or 11/11 is China's Black Friday. Alibaba has a huge sales and entertainment event on this day that goes by a variety of names such as the Double Eleven Shopping Festival, the 11.11 Shopping Festival, the Alibaba 11.11 Global Shopping Festival etc.

Young Males

Young male consumers, especially the post-95 generation, have become another consumption force. The growing economy and technology have led to expanded social and work lives. Unlike their fathers or grandfathers, they care much more about their appearance and personal image and are willing to spend more on hairstyles, clothing and fitness. They think a tidy appearance is essential for job interviews and dating. A remarkable increase in male grooming products has been noticed and the total consumption volume for male consumers is getting close to that of female consumers, especially in the online market. During Alibaba's 2017 11.11 Shopping Gala, searches for men's cosmetics more than doubled.

Young men in China spend an average of 24 minutes a day on their appearance. Of male consumers living in first tier cities, 88% regularly check out grooming, fitness and fashion information online and 83% of those between 18 and 35 think it is necessary to use skin care products.

The sales volume of male grooming products in China is growing rapidly and the total market volume of male grooming products in China is expected to reach 1.9 billion RMB (290 million USD) per year by 2019.

Women in Luxury

Globally, the luxury market is female-dominated but in China, it has been and still is male-dominated. In the past 5 years, however, consumption by women has been steadily increasing.

One of China's biggest online shopping platforms, JD.com, reports that the women's luxury market is currently worth 2.5 trillion RMB (390 billion USD) and is expected to grow to 4.5 trillion (702 billion USD) by 2019.

Luxury goods like handbags, watches and luxury cosmetics are becoming more popular, especially with younger, educated women with higher incomes. Affordable luxury brands have also gained popularity and built a reputation for high-quality design with relatively attainable prices. Though women are now more willing to spend on luxury goods, they're still price-sensitive. They do research before buying, make their choices carefully and feel that discounts and good offers are worth waiting for.

Chinese consumers are changing fast. They're trendsetters. They're demanding. They expect a lot. They know their power. They travel, study abroad, buy from overseas brands and export their expectations far and wide. Whether your business is already serving Chinese customers or not, it's important - for any business that's planning to be successful globally and relevant in the long run - to understand them and how they buy.

CHAPTER 3

The Chinese Consumer Trends You Must Understand

Consumption has become the primary driver of China's economy. Numbers from the National Bureau of Statistics show that in the first half of 2017 consumption not only accounted for 63.4% of China's economic growth, but also made up 57.3% of total GDP. Retail sales have grown at double-digit rates for years.

Online retail sales have grown from 3.8 trillion RMB (593 billion USD) in 2015, to 4.9 trillion RMB (765 billion USD) in 2016 to an estimated 5.6 trillion RMB (878 billion USD) in 2017. Brick-and-mortar vendors also saw huge jumps in sales volume. So, it's clear that Chinese consumers are buying more. But what are they buying and how? Let's take a closer look.

3.1 What Are They Buying?
Current Consumption Trends

With robust economic growth comes change in purchasing and consumption behaviour. In terms of product categories, there's been a significant shift from daily necessities to a wider group of products. There's also a remarkable trend toward guilt-free consumption of expensive, premium products.

Entertainment and Tourism

With more disposable income, people are spending more on entertainment. They visit restaurants, movie theatres and go to karaoke (KTV) more often and travel more. Travel and entertainment now represent 11% of monthly household spending, which is twice the level recorded in 2011.

Tourism has seen outstanding growth. Now more than ever, Chinese people are travelling. In 2016, there were 4.4 billion national travellers with year-on-year growth of 11%. Moreover, many of them show a strong willingness to travel abroad. The number of outbound travellers hit a record high at 122 million, with an annual increase of 4.3%. This area still holds huge potential.

Changes in Chinese travellers' behaviour has been noted in recent years. They're adapting more "Western" travel habits. Instead of just going sightseeing and shopping, they're more willing to engage in in-depth experiences of local lifestyle and culture. Unique, tailor-made travel services are also a new trend. For example, some are moving from 5-star hotels to boutique hotels or Airbnb homestays and bespoke tours are becoming more popular.

Health and Wellness

There's a new level of consciousness about health and well-being unfolding in China. This is not only reflected in purchase trends for the daily necessities of life, such as food, clothing and shelter, but also in new attitudes to physical health and more holistic views of the body, mind and soul.

Chinese people are very concerned about safety issues, especially in regard to food and products made for children. China has experienced a series of food safety scandals from 2006 onward. These incidents have involved fake food items, improper use of ingredients, unsafe additives, unhealthy production methods and contaminations. The food items affected have included meat, eggs, cooking oil, tofu and noodles. The most serious incident, the 2008 milk scandal, involved baby formula. People trust overseas suppliers more and try to source items online or from foreign sources when possible. Chinese parents have shown less trust in milk powder and milk products made in China and still prefer to buy imported milk powder from Special Administrative Regions like Hong Kong and Macau or from Australia and the U.S.

The increasing number of senior citizens in the country also contributes to this trend. A new custom is to buy health supplements as gifts for parents and grandparents on special occasions.

Pollution problems in major cities have also contributed to Chinese consumers pursuing healthier, greener lifestyles. Less labor intensive work and expanded personal lives also mean that people are more concerned about fitness and exercise. Surveys reveal that the number of people pursuing fitness is expected to exceed 10 million in 2017. This number has maintained an average increase of 10% in the past few years.

More and more people, especially the young, go to gyms and hire personal trainers for one-on-one coaching. Alternatively, they use fitness apps like Keep to make detailed fitness plans, follow instructional videos and buy fitness courses.

This trend is also reflected in WeRun, a step tracker within WeChat that includes a ranking system. As of September 2017, the number of daily active WeRun users had reached 115 million, with an annual increase of 177%. Every day, users "compete" with the aim of topping the daily leaderboard.

Growing health concerns have also boosted sales of smart devices like smartwatches that can count steps or measure your heart rate and electronic scales that can calculate body fat. Searches for exercise equipment more than doubled during the 2017, 11.11 Single's Day Shopping Festival.

Premium Products and the Luxury Market

You are what you wear and the impulse to show status with premium products is more and more evident in China. Many also believe that these products improve their lives.

Luxury products are a key high-end product category with significant growth. In 2016, 7.6 million Chinese households were estimated to have purchased luxury goods, each spending an average of 71,000 RMB (10,900 USD) per year. This is twice what households in legacy luxury markets such as France or Italy spend. In 2017, the market saw an incredible increase to a total market size of about 24 billion USD. The major reason is that a growing number of fashion-savvy Chinese consumers have started to purchase more at home, which has helped to boost sales.

Moreover, this market is due to grow in importance. The number of Chinese millionaires is expected to surpass that of any other nation by 2018, and by 2021 China is expected to have the most affluent households in the world. By 2025, the number of Chinese luxury consumers is expected to reach 150 million. Premium products and services are in demand.

At the same time, average Chinese consumers are now willing to pay for services that they have previously been unwilling to pay for and are also seeking out more specialized services. In the past, pirated DVDs were widely available in shops and pirated videos were widely available online. People were unwilling to pay the going rate for certain things.

These channels have now been closed off to a great degree, people are more willing to pay and lifestyles have also changed. For example, busy young people watch less television because they have tight schedules and spend more time hanging out with friends and colleagues. Instead, they use streaming websites like Tencent Video, iQiyi, Youku and LeTV. Users only need to pay a small amount each month for memberships that allow them to watch upcoming episodes that haven't aired yet. The market of paid membership services on these online video platforms is predicted to reach nearly 90 million in 2018.

Digital and Smart Devices

Consumers in China are much more tech-savvy than previous generations. They pay attention to trends and want the latest tech and newest models for practicality as well as fashion.

Purchases of wearable devices and smart household products in China increased by 19% and 18% respectively in 2017. About a third of urban Chinese consumers now own home or wearable tech.

Virtual reality (VR) is another market with huge potential. As VR is integrated throughout a variety of industries, GfK forecasts that retail sales of imaging devices including drones and VR equipment in China will grow from 650 million RMB in 2016 to 1.6 billion RMB (101 to 250 million USD) in 2017. Key domestic digital firms like Alibaba, Tencent and LeEco will continue to invest heavily in VR in the coming years.

3.2 How Are They Buying it?

The Online Consumption Route Map

With the development of technology and the growing e-commerce market, Chinese consumers are gradually decreasing their purchasing from brick-and-mortar stores and using e-commerce platforms more and more. This transition is spurring the continuing evolution of the online consumption ecosystem. Social media now also serve as search engines. One of the priorities for WeChat in 2018 is to increase its search function accuracy. With WeChat search, users can see the engagement between users and brands, what content brands published recently and the comments received on Moments pages, articles and official accounts. Other platforms like Weibo, Douban and Zhihu are also often used to find product information and user recommendations. Let's see how a typical Chinese consumer purchases online and what a uni channel experience is like.

Pre-purchase

The Search

The online search has become a key part of the purchasing process in many parts of the world. China is no different. Similar products, price and quality are all compared before consumers make their final decision.

In addition to domestic search engines like Baidu (百度) and Sougou (搜狗), Chinese consumers also search on e-commerce platforms like Taobao (淘宝), JD.com (京东), VIP.com (唯品会) and Xiaohongshu (小红书). For more niche categories, there are also vertical social platforms like QYER.COM (穷游) for travel and Babytree (宝宝树) for parenting and child care items.

Search results are updated in real time and customized based on data such as the user's search and browsing history. Some recommendations appear as display ads and platforms also show product and brand suggestions that are usually spot-on. This process often leads directly to purchases. About a third of Chinese consumers say they would purchase an item after seeing its ad, while fewer international consumers would. These ads also drive exceptionally high click-through rates and longer online visits on the platforms.

Peer Recommendations and Feedback

People in China attach great importance to recommendations from others and flock to social media platforms like WeChat and Weibo to check product feedback from peers, family and professional bloggers. The fan effect is strong in China and those who follow celebrities are likely to purchase items they showcase or recommend.

They also take comments from previous buyers seriously and check out their comments closely. Surveys have shown that most Chinese online consumers trust other buyers' comments. Almost half also leave comments about products they've bought online while global consumers are much less likely to do the same.

While Purchasing

Live Demos on E-commerce Platforms: See Now, Buy Now

Since 2016, live streaming has become a hit and e-commerce platforms like Tmall (天猫) and Mogujie (蘑菇街) developed a live streaming function that allows vendors to show their products to potential buyers in a more vivid way.

These live demos allow viewers to ask questions about the product and interact with other viewers through the comments. Vendors display their products, demonstrate how it's used and answer viewers' questions from time to time.

If a viewer is interested, he or she can click the item on the screen and purchase it immediately. This "See Now, Buy Now" mode offers a vivid experience for potential buyers and helps to shorten the conversion path.

Social Media: Buy What You See

Consumers may also purchase directly on social media platforms like WeChat and Weibo which allow users to embed purchase links from partnered e-commerce platforms. For example, on WeChat, you can embed links directly from JD.com and on Weibo, links from Taobao and Jumei (优品) can be added.

If people see something they like on these platforms, they can purchase them immediately by clicking these embedded purchase links. These "Buy What You See" opportunities take product placement to the next level and make the path from discovery to purchase seamless.

Mobile Payments and Immediate Distribution

Mobile payments speed up the online purchase process and are a key factor in the popularity of online shopping in China. The two most used mobile payment tools in China are Alipay (支付宝) and WeChat Pay (微信支付), developed by Ant Financial (Alibaba) and Tencent respectively.

Alipay and WeChat Pay are both easy to use. Users scan a QR code and then use their fingerprint or a password to confirm payment. Money is then automatically deducted from their digital wallet or a linked bank account. More advanced security measures, such as facial recognition, which was introduced by Alipay in 2017, ensure safety during transactions.

Once the payment is successful, express delivery service providers such as SF Express (顺丰速运), Cainiao (菜鸟) and JD Logistics (京东物流) play a crucial role in distribution. The logistics information is transparent and packages can be monitored online with a tracking number. In major cities, goods can be delivered within 15 minutes of the order being placed.

Post-purchase

Feedback

After the buyer receives the product, most e-commerce platforms encourage them to rate the product. At the same time, they can add comments as a reference for future buyers about the quality. They can also answer questions from potential buyers about their experience with the product.

If they're not satisfied with the product, buyers often contact the brand's social media account. Consumers can send an enquiry or make a complaint directly by leaving a comment under the brand's recent posts or sending a direct message. This is usually more efficient than making a phone call or writing an email.

Some professional bloggers regularly post product reviews on social media. They share their experiences, talk about pros and cons and rate the product or compare it to its competitors. Online shoppers often refer to these reviews before buying products.

Weak Brand Loyalty

Chinese consumers are not that loyal to brands. Rather, they're adventurous shoppers who are open to new products and brands. They're easily attracted by innovative offerings and creative multimedia content. A study conducted by Accenture revealed that roughly three fourths of Chinese respondents turned to new brands or suppliers during the year in 2016.

At the same time, more and more brands are entering China resulting in an even more fragmented market. Existing brands are at risk of losing once-loyal customers.

CHAPTER 4

How to Enter the World's Largest E-Market

You've decided it's time for your company to take its next big step. You're diving into the China market. It's attractive with huge potential. However, it's a unique, sophisticated and hyper-competitive market where it is not easy to succeed. In this chapter, we'll briefly talk about the three ways for a foreign brand to enter China and six major online sales channels for cross-border e-commerce.

4.1   Entry Models

Using a Local Distributor

Good local distributors have localization insights, specialist market knowledge and existing customers. They can give advice and help bring your products to market. You can partner with larger distributors or several smaller regional ones and cover most parts of China to build brand awareness. Local distributors can also handle customer service and product returns. This can reduce a brand's workload but controlling the quality of these services may be an issue.

Pros & Cons: Distributors have a vast network of established contacts to grow your business as well as a salesforce with access to the local market. They can hold inventory of your product in order to shorten the product to market lead time. However, some distributors have exorbitant markups and will price your product out of the market. And most of them won't share market and consumer information.

Establishing a Business Presence in China

There are five ways to establish a business presence in China. You can set up a Wholly Owned Foreign Enterprise (WFOE or WOFE, 外资企业) which is a limited liability company wholly owned by foreign investors. Establishing a Representative Office (RO, 代表机构办事处) is another option. They can engage in some liaison and promotional activities but can't directly engage in operational activities such as issuing invoices and receiving payments.

A Foreign Invested Partnership Enterprise (FIPE, 外商投资合伙企业) is an unlimited liability business entity with no minimum requirements on registered capital. It's similar to a WFOE, but enables partnerships and is popular with startups.

Joint Ventures (JVs, 合资) are limited liability companies formed between a Chinese and foreign company that share expenses, management and profits and losses. Authorities in China favour this model because it brings in new technology and skills while foreign investors value the low labor and production costs and a potentially huge market share. Businesses such as restaurants, bars, construction companies, automobile manufacturers and cosmetics producers are required to use this model.

Hong Kong Companies are often used as a Special Purpose Vehicle (SPV) to invest in a WFOE. Companies often manage their supply chains from HK because of its infrastructure, sound legal framework, efficient banking system, low taxation, convertible currency and qualified workforce.

Pros and Cons: Although there are a range of options available, it must be remembered that setting up any kind of business presence in China comes with substantial costs and a big commitment of time and resources. This option isn't advised for newcomers. It should only be explored after building a prominent online presence and an integrated distribution network.

Engaging in Cross-Border E-Commerce

Cross-border e-commerce (CBEC) is the process of purchasing products online directly from international retailers and suppliers that do not have a business entity in China. This kind of shopping is attractive because wealthy and middle class consumers want new items that aren't available in China yet. There's also a perception that products available on cross-border e-commerce platforms are higher quality and genuine because the brands are established and authorized abroad. On top of that, items are exempt from import taxes under certain conditions so prices can be significantly lower than for items imported the usual way.

CBEC is widely used in China. In 2017, the value of online cross-border purchases by Chinese consumers was estimated to be over 80 billion USD and growing. This is the most popular entry model and continues to grow but entrepreneurs need to stay alert for changing rules and regulations.

Pros and Cons: Cross-border e-commerce is popular and products from foreign companies are seen as better value, more reliable and exclusive. However, brands must set up an online payment gateway such as Alipay because international credit cards and payment systems such as PayPal are not widely used in China. Brands that are doing cross-border e-commerce must also invest in marketing.

4.2   Online Sales Channels

As mentioned above, cross-border e-commerce is the most popular entry model for foreign brands entering China. Before taking the next step, let's learn more about the major online sales channels in China to help you select the most suitable platforms for your brand and products. Currently, there are six options available for online sales in mainland China.

An Official Website Based Outside of China

Most international brands have their own official website that's set up outside of China. This makes it easy for the brand to manage and maintain.

However, this option has several major drawbacks. First, as the servers are not in China, it may be difficult for users to access. With the competition of large e-commerce platforms in China that online shoppers are used to, it's hard to drive traffic to the site. On top of that, without a legal business entity in China, they can't advertise using traditional channels.

Another huge disadvantage is the challenge in delivering customer service. As all the services are located outside of China, it's difficult for brands to provide quality after-sales service, refunds and product exchanges. The incompatibility with Chinese payment methods may also stop potential buyers from purchasing. There are also risks in the delivery process.

Pros and Cons: It's easy for brands to manage their own websites outside of China. But without hosting in China, the website will experience slow loading and display delays. Meanwhile, brands need to spend time and resources to build the whole buying journey for Chinese consumers, from payment to delivery to after-sales service.

An Outlet on a Popular Online Mall

There are large online malls that were developed in China such as Taobao, Tmall and JD.com which are extremely popular. They may seem like an easy option but let's look at how they work in reality.

There's a common misconception in the West that Taobao and Tmall are the same but that's not really the case. Taobao and Tmall are both operated by the Alibaba Group but they use different underlying models. Taobao is a C2C (customer to customer) platform for individual vendors while Tmall is a B2C (business to customer) platform for official manufacturers, brands or organizations that have a legal entity in China.

To open an online store on Taobao, Tmall or JD.com, you need to be a Chinese national or have a legal business entity in China. As an option for foreign brands and manufacturers who want to sell to China, both Tmall and JD.com have developed new platforms for cross-border e-commerce – Tmall Global (天猫国际) and JD Worldwide (京东全球购). They are also the most popular cross-border e-commerce platforms in China. Other platforms include Suning Global (苏宁海外购) and Amazon China Global Store (亚马逊海外购).

Pros and Cons: These platforms can provide a great deal of access, but online stores on these malls requires high setup fees and commissions. Brands may also need to pay extra advertising and marketing costs.

Brands can do a random search for their brand name on Taobao. If they find that there are already a number of daigous [traders selling to a small network] selling a good amount of their merchandise on a monthly basis, maybe it's time to think about China more strategically. A first cautious step for more risk-averse brand owners is cross-border e-commerce on Tmall Global or JD Worldwide."

—Mirko Wormuth from OmniChannel China

Online Hypermarkets

Unlike the online malls introduced above, online hypermarkets function on a B2B2C (business to business to customers) system. These online hypermarkets operate as intermediaries. They purchase a wide range of goods from overseas suppliers or manufacturers at wholesale price and sell them at retail making their profit from the markup.

They're different from online malls in a few ways. Online hypermarkets do not have individual online storefronts for overseas brands to manage. Storage and distribution are also managed by the hypermarket. Well-known online hypermarkets in China include NetEase Kaola (网易考拉海购) and Jumei.

Pros and Cons: Similar to number 2, while these platforms can provide a great deal of access, setting up an online store on these malls requires high setup fees and commissions. Brands may also need to pay extra advertising costs.

Vertical Specialty Marketplaces

These platforms operate like online hypermarkets and also purchase goods directly from overseas suppliers or manufacturers. However, they generally only focus on a specific product category, target audience or location.

As the product catalogue is limited, the market on such platforms is rather niche and the consumer traffic is relatively low. On the other hand, these platforms are quite popular with their target audience.

One example is beibei.com (贝贝), which is a specialty marketplace for maternity, infant and child care products. Xiaohongshu (小红书) is another example of this kind of cross-border e-commerce platform. It allows Chinese users to check out and purchase overseas products posted by other users, including cosmetics, skin care products, nutrition-related items, parenting products and more. In-depth product descriptions and reviews can also be found on the platform. Other popular specialty retail platforms include Mogujie and Meilishuo.

Pros and Cons: Similar to number 2 and 3, while these platforms can provide a great deal of access, setting up an online store on these malls requires high setup fees and commissions. Brands may also need to pay extra advertising costs.

Flash Sales Platforms

Flash sales platforms offer a limited number of new-to-market or surplus products at highly discounted prices for a brief time. These platforms are a good choice for overseas manufacturers or brands who want to test the reaction of Chinese consumers before mass producing an item or rolling it out on a larger scale.

At the same time, flash sales are an irresistible marketing technique that can lead to huge exposure. They're also a good way for a newcomer to earn some recognition at an early stage. The most well-known flash sales platform in China is VIP.com.

Pros and Cons: These platforms can provide a great deal of access and a large pool of customers. They may also help increase brand recognition. However, brands don't often make a profit on these sites and customers are sometimes reluctant to pay more after being introduced to a product at a discount price. Brands may also lose customers if they move to a different platform. Setting up an online store on these malls requires high setup fees and commissions. Brands may also need to pay extra advertising costs.

Social Media

WeChat is the most used app in China. Many brands and manufacturers have not only opened an official WeChat account for mass broadcasting and customer service but also set up their own WeChat store for direct sales on the platform.

The biggest advantage of a WeChat store is that it can be opened without a legal Chinese business entity. It's also good for CRM and sales promotion as it's integrated in the WeChat system and linked with an official account. However, WeChat is a semi-closed platform, which makes it a bit hard to grow followers in a short time.

While WeChat is the best known social media channel for China market entry, it's not the only one. Some brands enter through live streaming on Weibo and Tmall, while others work with bloggers that sell their products on commission.

As you can see there are plenty of options available for market entry, all with their pros and cons. But no matter which entry model is chosen, for brands who really want to make their mark in China, a thorough understanding of Chinese social media is essential.

The winning formula for international brands in China's cyberspace is go big, go niche, or go home. Succeeding online requires an excellent understanding of the populations you're targeting and coming up with a fantastic value they'll love you for. Learn from the Chinese digital native brands. Build your online value proposal around a relationship, not about a product or a brand. Be agile. Test ideas fast (1-2 months). Don't plan for a whole year ahead."

—Joseph Leveque, Managing Partner of 31Ten

CHAPTER 5

The Chinese Social Media Platforms You Need to Know

A major uniting factor in this large, diverse digital market is Chinese social media mania. Social media is not an option for marketing in China. It's a necessity.

With the stunning rise of mobile technology, more and more people are using social media to connect with each other, share their achievements and feelings, obtain information, voice their opinions and buy, buy, buy. This is especially true in China, where the average time spent on social media is 1 hour and 50 minutes.

Because of this, Chinese social media can work as an important entry point to the China market. To do this well, a brand's social media account should be thought of as a business branch.

> *Social is becoming an increasingly important lead generation channel. It's not uncommon for brands to have a lot more consumer interaction on their WeChat account than their website.*
>
> *However, having a minimal website presence is still recommended for the sake of credibility, SEO and control of what appears to people looking for your brand and product names online. Or at the very least set up a Baidu Baike page for your company."*
>
> —Joseph Leveque from 31Ten

5.1 Similarities and Differences in Social Media Usage: China versus the West

The main similarity between social media users in China and the West is that they both use social media primarily for instant messaging and to catch up on the latest news and entertainment.

However, for Chinese users, social media is also an e-commerce channel. They look for deals, discounts and special offers. Brands often give out coupons and free samples or hold lucky draws. Chinese consumers love these online campaigns and seek out the latest ones. They follow celebrities, famous bloggers and Wanghong (China's version of D-listers or people who are "internet famous") to check out the latest trends and look for purchase recommendations. Then, they make purchases on social media via integrated e-commerce stores.

Social media is also where consumers go when they have a question to ask or a complaint to make. It's quicker and easier than emails or phone calls and their problems can be fixed in only a few minutes. It's an effective CRM (customer relationship management) tool and can be used for branding. It can also be used as a test bed to check reactions to new products and make necessary adjustments.

5.2   The Chinese Social Media Landscape

Similarities and Differences in Social Media Usage

	Chinese	Western
Sharing moments from daily life	✓✓	✓✓
Connecting with friends	✓✓	✓✓
Instant messaging	✓✓	✓✓
Daily necessity services (eg. taxi hailing)	✓✓	✗
Following the latest news	✓✓	✓
Games	✓✓	✓
Reading long articles and educational information	✓✓	✓
Following celebrities	✓✓	✓
Participating in promotional campaigns	✓✓	✓
Collecting coupons and sales incentives	✓✓	✗
Looking for purchase recommendations	✓✓	✗
Direct purchasing	✓✓	✗
Payments	✓✓	✗
Contacting businesses' customer hotline	✓✓	✗
Work	✓✓	✗

✓✓ Used extensively   ✓ Used   ✗ Not used or rarely

Similar to the west, there are major platforms like Weibo, WeChat, Baidu and Taobao that dominate, but the overall digital landscape is fragmented.

Platforms are segmented by function - live streaming, blogging, image sharing etc. - or cater to niche audiences - movie lovers, artists, students etc.

Let's have a quick look at some of the major players in China.

The Big Two

WeChat (微信)

WeChat, known as Weixin (微信) in Chinese, started as a mobile instant messaging app but has grown to include features such as a Moments page, official accounts, WeChat Pay and a mini program platform. WeChat is the most used app in China. For brands hoping to step into China, opening an official WeChat account is a must. For the purposes of this book, the word "WeChat" refers to the Chinese version of the app by its English name, not to the international version, which is a bit different.

Sina Weibo (新浪微博)

Weibo is a microblogging platform. It's a Chinese hybrid of Facebook and Twitter and is a fast-flowing information source, trend spotter and trend setter. Brands have access to advertising options as well as campaign formats to promote on Weibo. You can also easily find the day's most discussed topics on Weibo and use them in your marketing strategy.

Weibo Integrated

Miaopai (秒拍) and Yizhibo (一直播)

These are the two most popular mobile apps for short video sharing and live streaming respectively. They are both partnered with Sina Weibo so users can view videos from these platforms directly on Weibo, which has strongly increased their exposure and popularity.

Short videos and live streaming have become two of the most popular trends on Chinese social media platforms. Short videos have taken hold because they can be shared easily without a need for huge bandwidth or memory. Live streaming exploded in 2016 with a big increase in the number of platforms, viewers and creators. Other major short video platforms include Meipai (美拍), Xiaokaxiu (小咖秀) and Kuaishou. Popular live streaming platforms include Inke (映客), Huajiao (花椒直播) and Douyu (斗鱼).

Other Major Players

Toutiao (今日头条)

It's a news aggregation platform that recommends news to individual users based on artificial intelligence that analyzes their preferences. It also allows individuals and media organizations to create official accounts to self-publish. Its user base has increased by leaps and bounds.

Zhihu (知乎)

Zhihu is the Chinese version of Quora, a question-and-answer website. Its slogan is "Share your knowledge, experience and thoughts with the world." On Zhihu, questions are created, answered, edited and organized by its users. In Classical Chinese, "Zhihu" means "Do you know?"

Douban (豆瓣)

Launched in 2005, Douban is an interest-oriented social network and UGC (user-generated content) platform focused on culture and lifestyle. It's a community site like Goodreads, IMDb, Blogger, Facebook, Pandora, Spotify, Ello and Fancy.com, but it's far more than that.

iQiyi (爱奇艺), Tencent Video (腾讯视频) and Youku (优酷)

These three platforms are the largest online video streaming sites in

China and the competition among them is fierce. In 2012, Youku merged with Tudou, another well-known online video website, and established the Youku Tudou Group which was acquired by Alibaba in 2016. But in recent years, Youku has witnessed a slowdown, leaving room for iQiyi and Tencent Video to join it at the top.

Bilibili (哔哩哔哩)

Known as "B Station" (B站) to users, this is a video sharing site for anime, manga and gaming fan videos. It allows users to add commentary that displays like subtitles except that they appear in scrolling ticker-fashion on top of the clips. Its niche content and unique commentary style distinguish it from other online video sites.

Another popular video platform for this audience is AcFun (弹幕视频网), which is an abbreviation of "Anime, Comics and Fun". Launched in 2007, it's also known as A Station (A站) but it's not as popular as Bilibili.

Douyin (抖音)

This is a music video social networking app for video creation, messaging, and live broadcasting. Users can select a piece of background music and film a short music video that lasts for 15 seconds. Its user base is young with about 85% below 24 years old. Douyin is similar to Musical.ly. In November 2017, Toutiao announced that it had purchased Musical.ly for about 1 billion USD and it plans to merge it with Douyin in the future.

Kuaisho (快手)

Founded in 2011, Kuaishou began as a gif-making and photo-sharing app. Then it gradually added short video creation and live streaming. Kuaishou claimed to have 700 million registered users as of November 2017. It's quite popular among young people living in third and fourth tier cities in China.

Ximalaya (喜马拉雅)

This is a well-known online audio sharing platform in China. Users can access all kinds of audio content including music, personal radio stations, audio books, radio dramas, paid audio courses, etc. By September 2016, Ximalaya had accumulated 300 million registered users.

Xiaohongshu (小红书)

Xiaohongshu, also known as "RED", literally means "Little Red Book". It's a fast-growing social commerce app. Users can discover high-end international products posted by members of the community and purchase them through their online stores.

It specializes in cosmetics, skin care, food, nutrition, maternity, child care, small appliances / electronics, household products and fashion. It's seen as a gateway to female consumers under 30.

CHAPTER 6

How Your Business Can Harness Chinese Social Media

To reach out to Chinese consumers and establish a closer relationship with them, a prominent presence on Chinese social media is a must for brands and companies, especially on the most popular platforms – WeChat and Weibo.

However, brands at different entry stages need to use different strategies due to their unique characteristics. Here three major business categories are presented with descriptions of effective ways for each group to use Chinese social media to its full potential. In later chapters, how to carry out these steps in detail will be discussed.

6.1 International Brands Already Established in China

This group includes brands that have already set up a legal entity in China. They have online shops, brick-and-mortar stores or both in mainland

China with local staff and an advanced understanding of the Chinese e-commerce ecosystem. These enterprises already have some brand recognition among Chinese consumers.

Platforms

For brands that are already established in China, a presence on WeChat and Weibo with verified official accounts is crucial. Many of them diversify their marketing channels and join specialty platforms that fit their industry. For example, Q&A platform Zhihu is favoured by many B2B brands like Siemens and IBM. As they're playing the long game, they're constantly on the lookout for new platforms where they can reach out to new consumer groups and get more attention. Emerging platforms, such as short video platforms like Kuaishou and Douyin, or live streaming platforms like Yizhibo and Inke, have many rising KOLs (key opinion leaders, influencers) who are open to brand promotion.

Functions

For these brands, customer relationship management (CRM) is the most important function, as social media is a fundamental part of Chinese consumers' personal lives. Marketing is another important function for engaging with consumers and promoting products and services. Sales can also be done on social media through channels such as WeChat Stores. For some brands it's an important channel to sell exclusive products that aren't being sold on their online outlets. Finally, brands need to keep an eye on new features and make the best of them.

Content and Community

Creating original and localized content is essential for brands to build an engaging and interactive social media profile. Brands also need to launch campaigns, engage bloggers for promotion and run advertising on a regular basis to build brand awareness and reach out to potential customers.

6.2 Brands Doing Cross-Border E-Commerce

As mentioned in Chapter 4, these brands sell to Chinese consumers via international retailers or suppliers. They don't have an intermediary business entity in China.

For those who want to enter China via cross-border e-commerce, six major online sales channels were introduced in Chapter 4. However, Chinese consumers may be reluctant to purchase your products when they see them on most of these channels because they likely know nothing about your brand. Therefore, a presence on social media is good for brand awareness and product promotion.

Prior to setting up an official account on major platforms, it may be more useful to engage key opinion leaders such as celebrities, bloggers, experts, etc. for some initial promotions.

Platforms

For brands that are doing cross-border e-commerce, they should have verified official accounts on WeChat and Weibo. They can also look into vertical platforms with a niche focus and e-commerce integration in order to promote products and expand their sales channels. Good examples of these are Xiaohongshu for fashion and beauty brands, Babytree for parenting products and Mafengwo (马蜂窝) for tourism.

Functions

One of the most important functions is to build a database of potential customers so that brands can communicate with them, build a community and sell to them on social media. Sales are important for these brands and products can be promoted on social media with links to e-commerce sites or other online retailers. In the long run, they might accumulate enough popularity on social media that a local distributor will approach them for cooperation.

Content and community

These brands can organize regular sales-driven campaigns to promote sales. KOL cooperation is a great marketing tool for these brands. They can pay KOLs to post brand information and product recommendations with links to online sales platforms. Sometimes, sales can be done through a KOL's personal online store as well.

6.3   Overseas Brands Serving Chinese Visitors

These brands are physically located outside of China. Their goal is not to sell their products to Chinese consumers while they're in China. Instead, they want to attract Chinese visitors to enjoy and pay for their services when they travel abroad. They are usually brands in the hospitality industry, such as restaurants and hotels, retail stores or schools that want to enroll international students. Distance makes it hard for Chinese consumers to get to know them so their biggest challenge is standing out from the crowd and getting noticed by Chinese outbound visitors.

Platforms

For overseas brands serving Chinese visitors, it's not necessary for them to have a presence on multiple channels. They should focus on WeChat and Weibo to engage with their target audience.

Functions

Marketing is the most important function for these brands to get exposure and promote their products or services to the right crowd. At the same time, they need to constantly build credibility with local communities and do word-of-mouth marketing in order to generate sales.

Content and community

Enhancing brand awareness and building credibility are the goals for many overseas brands. This can be done through blogger promotion, paid advertising, and sometimes running seasonal campaigns.

	Social Media Goals	Emphasis	Social Media Platforms
International Brands Already Established in China	Integration between all channels and platforms	CRM, marketing and sales	WeChat, Weibo, niche platforms (e.g. Zhihu, Douban), and emerging (e.g. Kuaishou, Douyin)
Brands Doing Cross-Border E-Commerce	Database building	KOL promotion and sales	WeChat, Weibo, e-commerce related platforms (e.g. Xiaohongshu, Babytree, Mafengwo)
Overseas Brands Serving Chinese Visitors	Enhancing brand awareness	Word-of-mouth marketing and KOL promotion	Weibo, WeChat and live streaming platforms (e.g. Yizhibo, Inke)

Big brands in China should strive for integration between all channels and platforms. Social media is an important part of this ecosystem primarily used for CRM and services, as well as a sales channel. Smaller companies doing cross-border e-commerce may have bigger plans to eventually open offline stores and local online stores, so building a database of Chinese customers is a priority along with sales. Overseas brands often benefit most from word-of-mouth, promoting user-generated content (UGC) and cooperating with KOLs.

PART II

WeChat: China's Operating System

CHAPTER 7

What is WeChat?

WeChat started in 2011 as Weixin, a free instant messaging app from Tencent, but steadily grew and continuously added functions. Inside China, it's used to do everything from ordering food and hailing taxis to paying for international flights. An international version called WeChat was then developed with some of the same functions but both systems use different server bases so there are some differences. For the purposes of this book, the term WeChat is used for the easier understanding of English speakers but it refers to Weixin as used within China.

By Q3 2017, Weixin and WeChat together had 980 million monthly active users. This was up 15.8% from a year ago. As of September 2017, around 902 million users on average logged in every day, which is an annual increase of 17%.

Chinese users rely heavily on WeChat. Over half of users spend more than 90 minutes on WeChat every day and it's used for work by 90% of users in China.

7.1 WeChat: A Day in the Life

Li Min is 24. She's a marketing manager in Guangzhou. On a typical day, WeChat plays an indispensable role. The first thing she does after waking up is tap on the WeChat icon on her mobile phone. She starts her day with WeChat by checking her Moments page where her friends and family share their lives to make sure she hasn't missed anything exciting.

It's breakfast time and Li Min loves reading during breakfast. She checks the long list of official accounts she has subscribed to and goes through all the news and push articles. Then it's time to go to work! Li Min takes public transportation to work every day and likes to use the shared bikes found everywhere in her city. She uses WeChat to scan the QR code on a bike and unlocks it by paying using WeChat Wallet. Piece of cake!

Li Min starts her workday by discussing a client's advertising campaign in her company's WeChat group and has a video conference using WeChat with colleagues who are on a business trip in Beijing.

It's lunchtime but Li Min was so caught up in her work that she forgot. She opens a mini program on WeChat, orders food and pays with WeChat Wallet. Her work colleagues, who need to finish some work, ask her to order something for them too and have already transferred money to her with WeChat Wallet.

Later in the afternoon, Li Min has finally finished a big task and needs a break. She opens WeChat to search for reviews of the watch she wants to buy. She was indecisive about it but now she sees lots of positive reviews and sales information from different sources. Now that she's made up her mind, Li Min opens another mini program for online shopping and makes her order. She also books flight tickets to go back home using a mini program. She's looking forward to seeing her parents after a long time away!

Later on, it's time to go home. It's been a long day but now she can do whatever she wants! She opens a WeChat mini program again to play a game with her friends after dinner. It's fun but tiring. She switches gears and checks her Moments page again. There's a post that catches her attention. Her friends have posted about donating to the Tencent Charity

Foundation. Li Min wants to join and donates some money from her WeChat Wallet after she reads the post and sends well wishes to her friend in a comment below the post.

This is a lot to handle so she decides to take a walk. After she comes back, she's surprised to find out that she's on the top of the WeRun rankings, for walking more than 15,000 steps that day and that this has been liked by a bunch of friends on WeRun.

Now it's time for bed. She shakes her phone to see if anyone interesting is online that she can chit chat with. Finally, she checks the weather using a mini program, then puts her phone down and falls asleep.

Connect and Share

Instant Messaging

In WeChat, users can send messages in text, voice message, pictures or video to their contacts and chat groups. They can also make audio or video calls. Links from other apps (QQ music, Weibo, Zhihu, etc.) can also be shared with WeChat friends either directly or through a group chat.

WeChat Shake (摇一摇)

This is an interesting function within WeChat that allows users to connect with others by shaking their phones at the same time. After that, they can add each other as friends and then chat.

Offline merchants like supermarkets and hotels can also use WeChat Shake to give out special offers. When users arrive at a designated location, they can open WeChat and shake their phones to get red packets or coupons.

TV stations have widely used this function to attract audiences and interact with them on a real-time basis. When people are watching a TV program, the "WeChat Shake" logo may pop up at the corner of the screen to remind them open WeChat and shake for red packets, gifts, or other special offers.

People Nearby

Just as its name implies, this function helps people find other users nearby. They can then add each other as friends and chat if they are looking for friends or someone to date. This function is based on their real-time location.

WeChat for Business Communication

WeChat is used in many workplaces and has developed a number of features, such as easy file sharing and conference calling options, to streamline it for work. As a result, it is used widely for intranet communication. Enterprise accounts are used more and more for things like applying for leave, tracking projects and submitting reimbursement forms. Since many Chinese people use WeChat heavily anyway, it saves everyone's time and money. It's also increasingly common for business people to scan each other's WeChat QR codes instead of exchanging business cards.

Moments

Moments is an important social networking function within WeChat. For general users, it works as a semi-closed platform where they can share text, pictures, short videos, articles and even external links. All the posts can only be seen by selected users.

It's also a significant channel for brands to promote themselves and add official account followers through Moments ads or other types of content shared by users.

Digital Wallet

WeChat Wallet: Red Packets and Paying Bills

Red packets with lucky money are a Chinese tradition on special occasions but they've now evolved into a digital form. Now with WeChat, red packets can be paid with one's WeChat Wallet balance or by account linked bank cards.

WeChat Wallet can also be used to settle bills by scanning a QR code or having one's own QR code scanned by merchants. Users can also transfer money directly to each other easily. There's even a "Go Dutch" function that makes it easier to pay for group activities such as team lunches.

Third Party Applications and Mini Programs

WeChat is also a platform for third party applications and there are mini programs for services such as paying for shared bikes, hailing and paying for taxis, paying electricity bills and more. Mini programs even allow users to shop online so they don't have to leave WeChat to use online shopping websites or apps.

Third party applications for booking hotels and flights also work smoothly within the app. Now that the App Store supports WeChat Pay as a payment method, iOS users can pay for applications or finish in-app purchases using WeChat.

A Finger On the Pulse

Official Accounts

A variety of official accounts established by brands, media or even individuals are available for users to subscribe to. They produce articles and that cover news, stories, product reviews and more. These update daily so people can get a lot of information through official account subscriptions. In the near future, WeChat has announced that it will be launching a dedicated app for official accounts, that is expected to provide expanded marketing opportunities for brands.

Information Mini Programs

If users already have a favourite newspaper or magazine, they can check for their mini program so that they can check for updates without leaving WeChat or switching to other media sources.

Search

Now that WeChat is improving its search function, information is becoming easier to find than ever. You can search for any content related to keywords, such as articles published by official accounts, mini programs, content published by your friends in Moments, conversation history, stickers etc. Users can do research on products they want to buy or find news on certain topics from the media, the public and their friends all within WeChat.

7.2   Weixin vs. WeChat International Version

Many people think that WeChat and Weixin are the same, and that Weixin is only the Chinese name for WeChat. This is part of the story.

This book details how to use WeChat (Weixin), the China-based version of WeChat. It is referred to by its English name - WeChat - to be clearer to native English speakers and readers.

WeChat (Weixin) is the version for users within China while WeChat's international version is designed for users outside of China. They don't belong to the same system or servers. Though they have similar interfaces and many common functions, the two differ from each other in several ways. Marketers seeking customers in mainland China need to be aware of these differences or they may end up targeting the wrong audience.

First of all, as mentioned above, WeChat (Weixin) and WeChat's international version target different user groups in different regions. WeChat (Weixin) operates in mainland China while WeChat's international version serves overseas users. When users download the app, the version is determined by the phone number used during your first login. You get WeChat (Weixin) from the China-based App Store or Google Play if your phone number and phone location are based in China and your phone user interface is Chinese. If not, you get the international version of WeChat.

Similarly, official accounts on WeChat's international version differ from official accounts on WeChat (Weixin). Since the Chinese and international versions use different servers, official account data is stored in different places. WeChat (Weixin) users aren't able to search for or subscribe to official accounts registered on the international version. They also can't participate in campaigns or promotions run by international official accounts due to strict internet regulations in mainland China. However, users of the international version of WeChat can search for official WeChat (Weixin) accounts and participate in their campaigns.

Previously, official accounts weren't permitted on Weixin for companies outside of mainland China but it was announced in early 2018 that businesses in Hong Kong, Macao, Taiwan, Korea and Japan can now apply for official accounts that will be visible on the app within the mainland. No further details are available at this time, however, on the application procedures or ultimate roll out date.

Another huge difference lies in the wallet functions (微信钱包) for the two versions. For example, in China, users can pay for a wide range of products and services with their WeChat (Weixin) Wallet, but these options aren't available to users of the international version of WeChat. Users of the international version of WeChat have more limited wallet functions except in South Africa. Foreigners living in mainland China, Hong Kong, Macao and Taiwan can also activate WeChat Pay accounts and link them with overseas credit cards. As regions outside of China use different currencies and have different financial regulations, WeChat international and WeChat (Weixin) depend on different third-party payment systems.

Other functions also differ slightly between the two apps. For example, the game centers in different regions show different games.

Therefore, foreign marketers need to distinguish between the two different versions. For those targeting mainland users, they need to register an official account on WeChat (Weixin) not the international version and go through the official procedures for activation and verification.

CHAPTER 8

WeChat's Working Model

As the most used app and most popular social media platform in China, WeChat has penetrated people's daily life. WeChat has a unique working model that covers everything from social networking to marketing, sales and CRM, but its heart lies in convenience. We'll explain this working model in more detail.

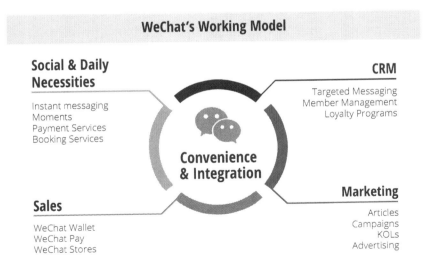

WeChat's Working Model

Social & Daily Necessities

Instant messaging
Moments
Payment Services
Booking Services

CRM

Targeted Messaging
Member Management
Loyalty Programs

Convenience & Integration

Sales

WeChat Wallet
WeChat Pay
WeChat Stores

Marketing

Articles
Campaigns
KOLs
Advertising

Social Networking and Daily Necessities

WeChat is fundamentally a social networking app with instant messaging as its core function. Users can send messages to their contacts and chat groups or make audio or video calls. In this sense, it's like WhatsApp and Line.

WeChat also has a popular social networking function which is officially called "Moments" in English but in actuality is called 朋友圈 ("Friends' Circle") by Chinese users. Users can update their status, share pictures or videos and post links to external websites. Their friends can like the post and write comments below it so the Moments page is like Facebook's wall and newsfeed.

In terms of daily necessities, users can use WeChat to pay utility bills, pay their mobile phone bill, order a taxi, book train and airline tickets and access a wide variety of city-based services for medical, transportation, housing and other issues.

Marketing and Advertising

Given the overwhelming popularity of WeChat in China, it can also be an excellent tool for marketing and advertising. In August 2012, WeChat launched official accounts (公众号). These allow enterprises, organizations, celebrities, governing bodies and media to broadcast messages or articles to their followers, in order to promote their brands, connect with individual users and improve customer loyalty. Users and fans receive regular updates and can have direct conversations with brands.

WeChat tries to integrate advertising into the user experience with its major ad types displayed in Moments and WeChat articles. The two types of ads differ from each other in their format, pricing model and minimum spend, which will be discussed in detail later.

WeChat is not a strategy. It's just a channel. It is only worth the consumer value proposal you build for it. And the key for it is to build a WeChat user journey as personal as possible, by understanding as much as possible who your follower is, what he/she cares about and how you can help."

— Joseph Leveque from 31Ten

Sales

WeChat is in the e-commerce arena with its very popular mobile payment system WeChat Pay (微信支付). Today, WeChat Pay and Ant Financial's Alipay (支付宝) occupy over 90% of China's mobile payment industry. Driven by the two mobile payment giants, China is gradually transforming from a heavily cash-based society to a largely cashless one.

Each user has a WeChat Wallet, which they link to their bank account to top up their wallet or transfer money. The wallet allows various kinds of transactions: purchasing all kinds of tickets (movies, trains, flights), paying utility bills, completing offline payments, transferring from banks or to friends, giving virtual red packets (红包) – monetary gifts in red envelopes which are given during holidays to friends or relatives - and so on. WeChat was the pioneer in making the tradition of giving red packets virtual.

WeChat also facilitates offline transactions by allowing brands to set up their own WeChat Pay account, so that customers can pay vendors via their wallet by scanning a QR code or showing their unique payment code. This is quick and simple for customers and vendors and has revolutionized the payment habits of Chinese consumers.

In addition, WeChat also supports WeChat stores that are integrated with official accounts so that users can finish their entire purchasing process within WeChat. If someone sees a product recommended in a brand's WeChat article, they can click on the WeChat store, add the item to their cart, pay with WeChat Pay and track the delivery. WeChat is an e-commerce ecosystem.

CRM

As a semi-closed platform, WeChat is good for customer relationship management (CRM), as it allows more intimate messaging between brands and customers. But CRM on WeChat is far more than that.

In addition to one-on-one messaging, WeChat offers other CRM functions like user demographics analysis for brands to develop a more in-depth understanding of their followers, template messages as service notifications and a custom menu bar, which directs users to access different services provided by the brand or helps them find the information they want quickly.

More sophisticated CRM systems can be integrated into WeChat, like chatbots that can be used to deal with simple enquiries, digital forms for user information collection, loyalty programmes and other advanced functions like food ordering services, hotel or restaurant booking and location-based navigation.

8.1   The Heart of WeChat: Convenience and Integration

Combining all these aspects above makes WeChat hugely convenient to use and makes a WeChat user's life much easier. People have the power to get almost anything done within WeChat and it's a touch point connecting the user to the world.

In January 2017, Tencent officially released its WeChat mini program platform. Mini programs are cloud-based embedded apps within WeChat which are simplified to retain their core functions. This means that users won't have to install as many apps as they do now. They don't need to take up precious phone memory and can store their data in WeChat's servers linked with their account.

In this way, users might one day do all their mobile activities within WeChat, without needing any other apps. In the future, people may only need WeChat installed on their phone.

To sum it up, WeChat has developed into much more than just an instant messaging app. In addition to social networking, it's strengthened its power in marketing, advertising, mobile payments and e-commerce. Targeting all these areas has enabled WeChat to gradually fulfill its ambition to be the ultimate operating system for life in China.

CHAPTER 9

How to Market on WeChat

9.1   Official Accounts

Given the omnipresence of WeChat in China, it's a key platform for marketing. A presence on the platform has become a necessity for brands. Sales, advertising, customer relationship management and many other marketing and sales practices can be carried out using only this platform.

Official accounts are the most important tool for marketing and advertising. They provide a channel for famous people, government, media and enterprises to promote themselves or their brands to millions of users. By Q3 2017, there were approximately 3.5 million monthly active official accounts and 797 million monthly active subscribers; an annual growth of 14% and 19% respectively. Stephen Wang, WeChat's Director of User Growth and Engagement, has said that the articles that a typical user reads each month equal a novel.

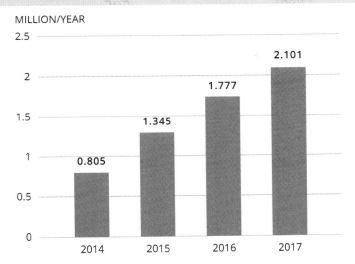

Number of official WeChat accounts (2014 - 2017)

Source: http://www.chyxx.com/industry/201712/594617.html

Three Major Types of Official Accounts

To start marketing on WeChat, the first step is to open an official account for your brand. Currently, there are three types of official accounts: Subscription Accounts (订阅号), Service Accounts (服务号) and Corporate Accounts (企业号). Each type has functions that meet different marketing needs.

Subscription Accounts

Subscription accounts are the most basic type of official account. They're designed primarily for updates and communication. Their major advantage is that they allow account holders to publish articles or send messages once a day. Each time they can publish 1-8 articles. This makes them a good choice for companies and media that are heavily content-based and update frequently. For individuals like famous people and bloggers, they can only open a subscription account.

These accounts are listed in the "Subscriptions" folder on the home page. Users don't get notifications when new articles or messages are published to minimize disturbance for those who follow numerous accounts.

Instead, a red dot, indicating an unread message, appears in the top right corner of the account's avatar. The number of unread posts is shown right under the account name. Users have to click into the folder to check out the latest updates. In the folder, all the accounts the user subscribes to are displayed according to their last update time.

Service Accounts

Service accounts offer more advanced features for businesses and organizations. For example, they have a more complicated CRM system that can integrate booking services, loyalty programs and even WeChat stores. They also support more advanced functions, such as speech-to-text conversion services, location-based services and WeChat Pay.

These accounts focus more on customer service and sales so they only allow account holders to broadcast four times a month. Each time, they can publish 1-8 articles. Unlike subscription accounts, service accounts appear in the chat list on the home page. Users receive a notification once articles or messages are published, like other messages from their contacts. This ensures greater visibility and also provides a feeling of familiarity.

All these features make service accounts an ideal tool for companies to build their own applications, facilitate interactions with customers and even establish an e-commerce platform for sales on WeChat.

Corporate Accounts

Corporate accounts are also known as "Enterprise Accounts". Unlike the two types of accounts introduced above, they are for internal communication within a company, instead of mass broadcasting to the public.

These accounts simplify the company's management and communication system. They are basically mobile OA (office automation) systems and can be used to record employees' attendance, establish department groups, send messages to staff and even encrypt messages in order to prevent confidential information from being leaked.

These accounts are closed communities, because only users with an invitation can access them. For external marketing purposes, you have to open a subscription account or a service account.

Tips

- It's best to open a service account unless you're a media company.

- As an international brand, you can register an official WeChat account in 3 cases:

1. You have a registered business entity in China.

2. You register with a local third party agent (2,000 USD) who will be the owner of your account.

3. You submit an application to WeChat directly and guarantee a minimum ad spend of 200,000 RMB (30,000 USD).

Basic Functions of Official Accounts

Official accounts provide all kinds of functions to help companies and brands do marketing.

Content Broadcasting

The most prominent function is content broadcasting. Articles and messages are the primary way that brands share information and communicate with followers on WeChat. There are five types of push content available: WeChat articles, text, images, audio and video.

Articles are the primary and most sophisticated type of broadcast content. An article can be made up of text, images, audio and video so it can be seen as a simple webpage.

At the bottom of each article, users can click to like it and check out the latest page views. The articles can also be shared on a users' Moments page as well as external platforms, like Tencent QQ, Qzone, Microsoft OneNote and EverNote.

In this way, even if a user has not subscribed to your account, he or she can still read your articles and find your account via this kind of cross-platform sharing. They can also reshare the articles so they're a great tool for marketers to create buzz.

As mentioned above, subscription accounts allow account holders to publish once every 24 hours, while the posting frequency of service accounts is much lower – four times per month, regardless of the content format. You can combine multiple articles and publish up to eight articles each time but no matter how many articles there are, they'll be presented as a single post on the user interface.

It's not a hard-and-fast rule that you should broadcast articles every day or include several articles each time. As long as you have enough resources and your articles are high quality, you can choose the frequency that suits your account type and needs.

In 2018, WeChat has announced that it will be rolling out a dedicated app for official accounts that will have extended functions and bring many advantages for merchants.

Comments Under Articles

In addition to liking and sharing, users can leave comments under the articles.

After users write a comment, it's not displayed immediately. Comments are collected for review on the management backend and will only be shown when the account holder moves it to the "Featured Comments" section.

Account holders are also allowed to reply to these comments. If there's a reply, it'll also become a "Featured Comment" automatically. Replies from account holders are displayed under the original comment and can be seen by everyone.

Choose interesting comments to respond to in order to let users feel appreciated and keep the conversational tone high. This inspires users to leave more comments and also gives official accounts another way to monitor and control comments shown to the public.

Automatic Messages

To improve communication efficiency, official account holders can create automatic messages. These messages can be sent in the form of text, images, voice messages or videos.

1. Welcome Messages (被添加自动回复)

A welcome message is automatically sent from an official account after a user subscribes to it. It can be text, a picture, a voice message or a video. Welcome messages say hello to new subscribers and provide a brief introduction to the account and its basic functions.

2. Auto-reply Messages (消息自动回复)

These appear when a user sends a message or enquiry to the official account. It can be text, a picture, a voice message or a video. Users receive auto-reply messages within an hour.

Generally, account holders leverage this function to let users know that they've received their message and will reply as soon as possible.

3. Keyword Auto-replies (关键词自动回复)

The keyword auto-reply function is more sophisticated. A designated reply appears only after users send a message that contains certain keywords. The rules can be pre-set by the account holder. Users will keep receiving auto-replies for each message that fits the rules.

This is very useful for FAQs (Frequently Asked Questions) as rules can be set up that correspond to each type of question. When users send a message that contains the keyword for a specific question, they receive a message that either contains the answer or links to another page that has the information they're looking for.

One-on-one Communication

Users that follow official accounts may send direct messages to ask questions, seek help, make complaints or give suggestions. It provides a channel for companies and brands to build a direct rapport with users.

Users in China prefer to chat with companies and brands directly via official accounts rather than sending emails or making phone calls,

because it's more efficient and private. From an account holders' perspective, WeChat is essentially a CRM system, whereby they can collect feedback directly from users and deal with their enquiries.

To contact a company or brand, users can send private messages to an official account. In addition to auto-replies, brands can also send messages manually for a "live chat". The sender is notified immediately when the official account sends a reply with a notification.

In WeChat, messages sent to your official account by users can not be replied to after 48 hours. This means that new messages must be checked on a regular basis and responded to quickly. In addition, messages are only retained in the system for 5 days.

Users expect a prompt reply from an official account, especially if their enquiry is urgent. Handling users' messages in a timely, professional manner plays a crucial role in official account management.

Custom Menus

Official accounts can set up a custom menu at the bottom of the account page. Each official account is allowed to add three main menus and five submenus under each main menu.

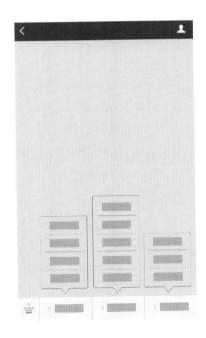

When users click on different menus, they receive various messages or WeChat articles, or will be directed to external web pages or mini programs.

Custom menus are particularly useful for service accounts as more complicated CRM systems can be integrated and different menus can be used for advanced functions like making bookings, loyalty programs and WeChat stores.

User and Content Analysis

The account management centre provides a variety of data related to account subscribers, including the number of subscribers and their demographics.

Moreover, account holders can track their content performance. They can see the article reach and page views as well as more detailed data such as the number of article shares and hyperlink clicks.

Tips

- Publishing 1-3 articles at a time is the optimal frequency for the average WeChat user. List the articles in order of importance.

- A custom menu should include the following information: a brand and product introduction, sales channels, contact details and customer service channels.

- Backend user data can be linked to the brand's own CRM system or sales conversion tools for better user data tracking and profiling.

9.2   Content Strategy

With an official account, you can reach your audience and grow followers by publishing content regularly. The success of an account is determined primarily by its content, and its ability to win the hearts of its customers. A well-designed account with valuable content can help it stand out from the crowd and connect with an audience.

WeChat articles are generally longer and more informative than posts on other social media. Users are more interested in content with useful, in-depth information and are also more likely to share it. Emotionally appealing content, brand news and discount updates are also very effective.

The most popular content types on WeChat fit into the following five categories:

Hot Topics

Hot topics are the most important content type to incorporate into your articles. They can be about a recent film or TV series, celebrities, books, buzzwords, special occasions, social issues, etc. Every day there are plenty of issues being discussed on social media so pick ones that are recent, relevant and local.

Relating an article to trending topics helps grab attention, encourage readership and stimulate sharing. Most organic followers find your account after seeing content that has been shared on their friends' Moments pages so it's extremely important to create unique, shareable articles that add character to your brand profile.

Hot topics can easily be found using Weibo or major Chinese search engines. However, they change rapidly from day to day so it's important to stay tuned in. Brands often leverage hot topics related to their product or industry and create articles about them as quickly as possible.

Useful Information

Users also like articles that teach them something helpful and are more than willing to share them to their friends and relatives. So this kind of post usually has relatively high engagement and can bring in a lot of traffic.

For example, practical tips, tutorials or extensive lists are popular on WeChat. Brands often give useful tips on how to use their products. This kind of content also helps brands show that they are professional and can enhance their credibility. Subscribers want to know that you're an expert in your field and that your account is a good place to get detailed insights into your products and industry.

Interactive Content

Lots of official accounts interact with their followers by telling jokes, sharing opinions, asking them questions, inviting them to participate in discussions, collecting their opinions on a specific topic, or creating a poll to let them vote.

This kind of interactive content helps trigger discussion and increases the account's exposure. However, this kind of interactive content should be created after the account has a few thousand followers or there won't be much interaction.

Sales

WeChat articles often contain basic information about sales promotions. However, this information is embedded in articles about larger topics because users are turned off by hard sales approaches, which are already omnipresent in their daily life. If the whole article is just for product promotion or like a dry newsletter, it won't hit the right notes with the audience.

Sales information should always appear with other types of content. For example, the article can start with practical tips on how to use their product, end with sales information and have other useful content in the middle. Purchase links or QR codes can also be added to facilitate sales.

Brand-related Content

Brand-related content includes authentic brand stories and news. It's a good idea to produce some articles about both the history of the brand and their latest achievements. This allows users to deepen their understanding of the brand which leads to enhanced brand loyalty.

Companies can also discuss recent product developments to keep followers intrigued and create anticipation.

Tip

- Most articles contain several content types. They may start with a trending topic, then have some educational information or fun elements followed by sales information at the end.

9.3   Promotion

Launching campaigns on WeChat is the most effective way to increase user engagement. Though WeChat itself doesn't have a function to organize campaigns, brands can still launch them via articles with incentives like discounts or giveaways. There are four comn campaign types on WeChat and that are often combined.

Lucky Draw

Lucky draws are the most common campaign type on WeChat. Generally, at the end of a WeChat article, a topic is raised for discussion and readers are encouraged to leave a comment or send a private message to the official account. Then the account holder can choose lucky draw winners from the participants. Lucky draws are quite effective in encouraging user interactions, attracting new followers and increasing their loyalty.

UGC (User-generated content) Collection

Brands can encourage users to create something, like a themed photo of themselves with the brand's merchandise, and submit it via private message to the brand's official account or upload it to a campaign page to win a gift. Sometimes brands also launch polls for users to vote for their favourite or pick the best ones to be featured in a future advertising campaign. Brands can also cooperate with KOLs who will encourage their followers to participate.

This type of campaign is another kind of lucky draw. The core difference is that visual user-generated content is more persuasive than written testimonials. It helps brands collect high-quality original content from their followers that can be used in other marketing activities and increases user engagement. It's also good for attracting new followers.

H5 Pages and Games

H5 pages, mobile-friendly webpages made with HTML 5.0, have become one of the most popular tools for WeChat campaigns. An H5 page can feature audio, video, complex animation and 3D effects. Many brands have integrated H5 pages into their WeChat articles to create campaigns. They allow brands to maximize visuals and interactivity to attract users.

The most common practice is to create a mini game with top players receiving a special gift. Alternatively, some brands create H5 pages that allow users to create sharable, individualized content, such as a page enabling photos to be viewed with special effects or in a new format.

H5 pages improve audience engagement and interaction. They have the potential to go viral and help brands achieve wider exposure on WeChat.

> *It's a very popular trend for companies to build H5 pages for event invitations, interactive digital product brochures, branding and other marketing purposes."*
>
> —Sheng Pang, CEO of Juplus Digital

Sales Campaigns

There are several ways to launch a sales campaign on WeChat. Brands can include themed coupons in WeChat articles that can be used online or offline. Before the coupon expires, users receive a message reminding them to use it. This establishes two touch points with users - upon collection and before it expires - making it a favourite with marketers.

Brands can also launch flash sales campaigns (a discount sale of designated items for a limited time), offer benefits for purchases over a defined amount or sell limited editions at a special price to boost sales.

Sales campaigns on WeChat help drive traffic offline or from official accounts to online stores. People love discounts and special offers so sales campaigns are also a great way to attract new followers and increase brand loyalty.

6 Tips for Launching a Campaign on WeChat

1.   Give each campaign a clear focus and objective. It can be to increase brand awareness, to boost sales or to collect user information and build a database. Before launching a campaign, first determine its goal.

2.   Offering incentives is a key way to achieve higher engagement. The more complicated the campaign rules are, the better the gifts should be. Offer gifts that are related to your brand, industry or the theme of the campaign.

3.   Choose a suitable duration for the campaign. A WeChat campaign usually lasts for one week in order to achieve optimal exposure and generate participation.

4.   Launching campaigns for festivals, special events or based on trending issues increases exposure and attracts a bigger audience. Weekends and holidays are the best times to launch campaigns. To make sure you don't miss any important days for promotion, create a marketing calendar highlighting major holidays like Chinese New Year, the Dragon Boat Festival, Mid-Autumn Festival, etc.

5.   For H5 campaigns, always test them prior to the launch and monitor them during the campaign for technical problems or bugs that might allow cheating, especially for campaigns that offer prizes and incentives.

6.   Regulations for campaigns on WeChat are strict. Brands can't launch any campaigns that ask people to follow certain WeChat accounts in return for incentives.

9.4   KOL Cooperation

Engaging influencers, known as KOLs (Key Opinion Leaders) in China, is one of the most effective ways to promote an official account, content or campaigns on WeChat. KOLs have their own follower bases who see their opinions and suggestions as credible and influential. Many also excel in driving online sales. Sharing brand information or launching campaigns with bloggers can help to raise brand awareness, attract new followers and contribute to a brand's credibility. Unlike bloggers in some other regions, it's not unusual for them to engage in direct sales.

With the expansion of official WeChat accounts, their followers continue to grow, increasing the influence and value of KOLs. Compared to WeChat's official advertising options, KOL promotion is often, but not always, more efficient and less costly.

On WeChat, the price of KOL cooperation differs primarily based on their industry, interest category, follower base, content quality and the prominence of their posts. The more followers, the higher the content quality, the higher the cost of a contract.

Types of KOLs on WeChat

Most KOLs have subscription accounts and can be found by searching within WeChat. They have official accounts that can be divided into 2 broad categories: individual accounts and agency-managed accounts.

Individual Accounts

Individual accounts are, exactly as the name suggests, created and managed by individuals. They can only open subscription accounts and WeChat doesn't verify accounts opened by individuals. They have a good rapport with their followers and are seen as reliable authorities when they recommend brands.

These bloggers also have stricter standards when selecting brands to cooperate with because they need to maintain their reputation and content quality. If a brand cooperates with an established individual account blogger, they can attract a sizeable audience and increase current customer loyalty.

Examples of popular individual accounts include 猫力乱步 (WeChat ID: maolispace), 郭姐哒 (WeChat ID: realsisterguo) and 阿滋楠 (WeChat ID: azinannan).

Agency-managed Accounts

These accounts are managed by an agency or a company that is listed on their profile page. Most of them are verified and sometimes there are several verified accounts under the same name. WeChat allows a maximum of 50 official accounts to be verified under one company name. These accounts are generally open to advertising and are more likely to accept hard sell advertising approaches on behalf of brands.

If an agency has several official accounts, brands can consider advertising on more than one account. Usually agencies offer discounts if brands choose more than one of their accounts to advertise on.

Examples of agency-managed accounts include 企鹅吃喝指南 (WeChat ID: qiechihe), 日食记 (WeChat ID: rishi-ji), 每天只种一棵草 (WeChat ID: yourshoppinglist)

On WeChat, micro-KOLs typically have less than 10,000 views. Mid-tier KOLs average around 50,000 views and top-tier KOLs have over 100,000 views."

—Kim Leitzes, Founder and CEO of PARKLU

Prices and Payments

WeChat KOLs are generally more expensive to work with than Weibo KOLs. Micro-KOLs on WeChat usually charge between 3,000 to 15,000 RMB (474 to 2,370 USD) per article. Mid-tier KOLs are likely to ask for a price ranging from 15,000 to 80,000 RMB (2,370 to 12,640 USD). The most popular KOLs on WeChat charge much higher, from 80,000 to 500,000 RMB (12,640 to 79,000 USD). Asking a KOL to create text, visual or video content or place the brand's post in a prominent position commands higher prices.

The majority of KOLs and their agencies take payments through Alipay. Bank transfers are also accepted but not preferred, as it usually takes a longer time to clear so it's best to open an Alipay account before doing any KOL promotions. Most bloggers in China require 100% prepayment and will only begin promoting after payment has been received.

For small-scale cooperations, with a contracted amount below 15,000 RMB (2,370 USD), bloggers rarely sign official agreements. The usual procedure is to negotiate the terms and pay the full amount prior to the work commencing. Please note that most individual bloggers do not issue legal receipts, called "fapiao" in Chinese, unless you request one. A legal receipt costs approximately 10% on top of the contract amount.

Finding KOLs on WeChat

While WeChat doesn't have a section where all bloggers are listed, there are three ways to find KOLs on WeChat:

WeChat's Native Search

Type keywords in the search bar and choose to only show results for official accounts. Then you'll see a list of official accounts based on the search keyword.

KOL Search Engines

There are various KOL search engines such as Sougou Search Engine for WeChat, Robin8, NewRank and gsdata.cn. Users can search for KOLs based on keywords and categories. Filters are provided to help further narrow the search.

With the help of these databases, users can easily get the latest data on the number of followers, total article views and other important statistics. Sometimes the price range of these KOLs is revealed too.

Another alternative is PARKLU, which is a KOL matchmaking platform where brands can outline their campaigns, budget and timeline, then choose KOLs who have applied for collaboration.

KOL Agencies

There are three major KOL agencies in China. They are Louis Communication (楼氏传播), Gushan Culture (鼓山文化) and Yaxian Advertising (牙仙广告). In addition to these, there are also many companies that manage KOL databases. Users can select KOLs by industry or interest category and promotion budget. They can also check their follower numbers and get quotes.

Auditing a KOL

After you've identified matching KOLs, you should check their previous articles to see the average article views, likes and comments. You can also ask the KOL to provide screenshots of their account performance statistics from their account management page to get a better idea of their audience and reach.

Working with KOLs on WeChat

WeChat KOL promotion is effective thanks to their large follower bases and their credibility. People feel comfortable buying based on KOL recommendations. When working with WeChat KOLs, you can decide which promotional method works best to maximize your branding and marketing goals. There are five common ways to work with KOLs on WeChat:

Advertorials or Product Placement

Advertorials (or native advertising) are the most common way for brands to work with WeChat KOLs. KOLs write an article about a topic in their usual style that features the product or use images featuring the product in the article. Since the articles are original, informative and interesting, readers are less likely to click away.

For a sales campaign, brands can ask KOLs to insert a sales link at the end of the article. More and more brands integrate different tracking codes in the purchase links distributed to different KOLs to measure their effectiveness and calculate the final commission based on a PPS (pay per sale) pricing model.

EAZYPEZY, a Chinese cashmere designer brand, cooperated with fashion blogger 黎贝卡的异想世界 (WeChat ID: Miss_shopping_li) in December 2017. She wrote an article about getting presents for her family, recommended the brand and included visuals of the clothes. At the end of the article she shared a special tracking code from EAZYPEZY and received more than 100,000 views.

Product Reviews

For brands, this is the most straightforward way to introduce their products and services. Many WeChat KOLs are experts in their field who produce informative, reliable product reviews and comparisons, so their followers consider them trustworthy.

Their product reviews are often paired with giveaway campaigns or links to the product's online sales page. Brands that partner with WeChat KOLs who like their products can reach a large audience and see a noticeable uptick in sales.

ARTISTRY, a cosmetic brand from the United States, also cooperated with 黎贝卡的异想世界 (WeChat ID: Miss_shopping_li) in January 2018 and invited her to write a product review, test their new lipstick and provide an online sales link at the end of her article. The article was viewed more than 100,000 times.

Sponsored Campaigns

Brands sponsoring KOLs to launch campaigns is another common practice. KOLs introduce the campaign and offer gifts sponsored by the brand. They can also direct traffic to the brand's official account by integrating the brand's official account QR code at the end of the article.

6ixty8ight, a fashion and lingerie brand for young women, cooperated with lifestyle blogger HelloDaH (WeChat ID: realhellodah) in August 2017. She posted photos of herself wearing lingerie and encouraged followers to comment in order to win some items from 6ixty8ight. The article was viewed more than 34,000 times.

Co-branding and KOL Crossover Promotion

Sometimes, brands co-create a product with a KOL and sell it as a limited edition. A great example of this is the co-branding between Mr. Bags (WeChat ID: bagsbaoxiansheng) and Givenchy at the beginning of 2017. 80 limited edition bags worth 1.2 million RMB (189,000 USD) sold out in 12 minutes. After this successful campaign, Mr. Bags did similar co-branding ventures with other luxury brands such as Burberry, Tod's and Chloe.

Sales on KOLs' WeChat Stores

More and more fashion KOLs have their own WeChat stores or mini programs for e-commerce purposes. Brands can offer special editions of their products in the KOL's WeChat stores.

Kitayama, an original bag brand from China, cooperated with the popular fashion blogger gogoboi (WeChat ID: realgogoboi) to sell items through his online store 不大精选.

Tips

- It's important to work together with KOLs so that they can retain their voice, style and approach while engaging in promotional ventures.

- Work with lots of KOLs for your first campaign to establish a baseline for results. Choose the top performing KOLs for your next campaign. Repeat this process until you're left with 3-5 bloggers that you work with regularly. It's best to work with quality bloggers long-term. If you work with effective KOLs again and again, their fans will get used to your brand and products and will act on promotions, follow your official account and more.

9.5   WeChat Advertising

Due to the personalization of digital advertising in China, Chinese consumers are twice as likely to click on an ad compared to the global average. Given its huge number of active users, WeChat has become a battlefield for advertisers to showcase and promote their products. But advertising is not open to all official accounts or all industries. Only brands with verified official accounts in specific industries can apply to become WeChat advertisers.

Currently, WeChat offers two major advertising options, namely Moments Ads (朋友圈广告) and Account Ads (公众号广告). A new advertising option for mini programs is currently in testing mode.

Moments Ads

As mentioned previously, the Moments page is similar to Facebook's wall and newsfeed. It allows users to share their status, photos, articles, etc. with their WeChat contacts. The ads here look like normal Moments posts but with an additional "Sponsored" tag in the upper right corner.

Moments ads can be used to promote an official account, publicize a campaign, encourage users to download an app, distribute coupons or launch location-based promotions. For Moments ads, advertisers can define their target audience by gender, age, location, industry, marital status, education level, and so on.

Display Formats

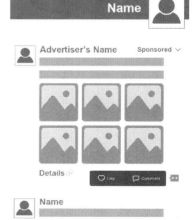

From 2017 on, Moments ads have two new formats. One is a card format with a larger space for visual elements. This enlarges the ad, making it more visible and eye-catching and also enables it to convey more information. Clicking the card directs readers to an H5 page or a native advertising page, shortening the conversion path.

The other one is an advanced card ad format with two buttons which enables advertisers to showcase two sets of advertising materials in one ad. Users can click on either button to view different advertisements.

Moments ads allow mutual interactions between brands and users and they can like and comment under the ad. WeChat is also testing a new function that allows brands to reply to comments left by users. In late May, 2017, TripAdvisor launched a Moments ad, which allowed users to ask questions by leaving comments.

Pricing

Moments ads adopt the CPM (Cost Per Mille) pricing model. Advertisers are charged per thousand impressions. There are also two purchasing schemes: **scheduling** and **auction**.

Scheduling	Auction
Scheduling ensures a certain amount of exposure based on the allocated budget	Auction is suitable for advertisers who need flexible advertising time and constant ad customization (not available for video ads)
CPM pricing model	CPM pricing model
Price depends on location: core cities, large cities and others: • RMB 50-150/M (8-24 USD) for Text, Image ad • RMB 60-180/M (9-28 USD) for Video ad	Price depends on location: core cities, large cities and others: • RMB 30-300/M (5-47 USD) for both Text, Image ad and Video ad
Minimum budget	Minimum budget
50,000 RMB/campaign (7,900 USD)	1,000 RMB/day (158 USD)

Account Ads

Alternatively, WeChat offers another advertising channel – account ads. Currently, there are three major types of account ads: footer ads, video ads and exchange ads.

Like Moments ads, account ads can also be used to promote an official account or a campaign, encourage users to download an app or distribute coupons. Account ads also allow brands to advertise products from their WeChat store so that users can find out more or directly purchase the item by clicking the ad.

Display Formats

There are 3 kinds of display formats. Footer banner ads appear at the bottom of a page after an article with a call-to-action button. Pre-roll video ads appear before videos. They can't be longer than 15 seconds and the video must be longer than 5 minutes for the ad to appear. There's also a "Learn more" button in the bottom right corner that takes users to another landing page for further information. Exchange ads are similar to footer ads. The major difference is that exchange ads may be presented in a larger card format with a call-to-action button.

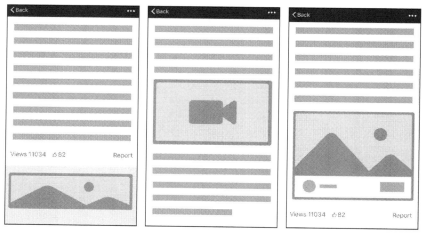

Footer Banner Ads   Pre-Roll Video Ads   ExChange Ad Cards

Pricing

Format	Scheduling	Auction
Footer banner ad	CPM pricing model. Price depends on location: core cities, large cities and other: • RMB 15-25/M (2-4 USD) Minimum budget: 1,000 RMB/campaign (158 USD)	CPC pricing model Minimum bidding price for each click is 0.5 RMB (0.07 USD)
Pre-roll video ad	CPM pricing model. Price depends on location: core cities, large cities and other: • RMB 15-25/M (2-4 USD)	CPM pricing model Minimum bidding price for thousand impressions is 10 RMB (1.60 USD)
Exchange card ad	Price to be confirmed by the account holder	Price to be confirmed by the account holder

Mini Program Ads

WeChat has recently released a new feature for its mini programs — allowing advertisers to bid for ad space in the "Mini Programs Nearby (附近的小程序)" section. However, it's still under internal testing and WeChat hasn't officially announced detailed prices or procedures.

When users open the "Mini Programs Nearby" list, they can see a list of mini programs based on their current location. With this new feature, advertisers can bid on ad space on this list.

These mini program ads also appear when people use the search function. For example, when users search for related keywords like "hotel", related mini-programs appear.

WeChat's advertising options allow marketers to choose the option that suits their promotion goals and budget best and to their products to filtered target consumers. They also offer an effective way to increase brand exposure and accumulate new subscribers.

And don't forget that Chinese audiences prefer meaningful content so creating quality ads remains the most important step in your overall WeChat advertising strategy.

Tips

- Moments ads are very effective for well-known brands with visually appealing products.

- Account ads serve businesses with active e-commerce sites well as clicking on the banners brings potential customers right to them.

CHAPTER 10

How to Start Selling on WeChat

In China, e-commerce is highly integrated with social networks. This trend has influenced both social and e-commerce platforms. WeChat Wallet is a prime example. This chapter gives a more detailed introduction to this powerful and widely used tool and shows how it can help boost your business.

10.1 WeChat Wallet for General Users

As mentioned before, each WeChat user has a personal WeChat Wallet that they link to their bank account to top up or transfer money from one to the other. With their WeChat Wallet, users can engage in the following kinds of transactions.

Money Transfers and Sending Red Packets

The most common use for the wallet is to transfer money to other WeChat users or send red packets. As mentioned before, red packets are a Chinese custom of giving small amounts of money to friends and family in red envelopes at Chinese New Year. WeChat made this tradition mobile and virtual in 2014 and soon after, WeChat Wallet users increased by millions.

Red packets have evolved and are now sent on various kinds of special occasions or as a quick way to transfer smaller sums to friends. In 2017, on average, people sent 28 red packets or 580 RMB (91 USD) each month. They also sent 46 billion red packets during the Spring Festival (aka Chinese New Year) in 2017, and over 6.4 billion were sent during the Mid-Autumn Festival in the same year.

Brands can also leverage this function as official accounts with a WeChat Pay account can send red packets to their followers on special occasions.

Daily Tasks

Besides money transfer and red packets, WeChat Pay provides a wide range of payment services. For example, users can use WeChat Wallet to repay credit card debts, purchase financial products and donate to charities.

Utility bills - phone, water, electricity, fuel and TV - can be paid with it as can parking and traffic tickets. It can also be used for city services such as making an appointment with a doctor, settling tax bills, etc.

Third-party Operators

In WeChat Wallet, there's a section at the bottom that says "Powered by third-party operator (第三方服务)". In this section, some major e-commerce, transportation, hospitality and tourism brands are featured. They are Tencent partners and this section brings them traffic and gives users a streamlined payment option.

For example, partner JD.com has its own section which allows users to access their online store from within the wallet. Other well-known brands featured here include popular taxi-hailing service Didi (滴滴打车); LY.COM (同程旅游), for flight and train bookings; eLong (艺龙旅行网), a leading online travel agency; Dianping (大众点评), which offers business information and group buying services; online food delivery platform Meituan (美团) and Mogujie (蘑菇街), a social e-commerce platform for fashion.

By partnering with these brands, WeChat has successfully established a comprehensive service network and cemented its presence in the daily life of Chinese users.

Since the end of 2016, WeChat has opened up its cooperations beyond partnerships, investors and stockholders. These new partners are listed in a separate section labelled "Limited time promotion (限时推广)", and are featured for a short period of time.

Starbucks was the first brand to benefit. At the end of 2016, customers could pay via WeChat in over 2,400 Starbucks stores across China. Then in early 2017, WeChat and Starbucks co-organized an O2O campaign called "Say it with Starbucks (用星说)". Users could buy gift cards by clicking a Starbucks icon displayed in their wallet and send them to friends in messages. The cards granted holders a free coffee in any Starbucks store in mainland China.

Later, Mobike (摩拜单车), a station-less bike-sharing system, partnered with WeChat. The Mobike button in the wallet is linked to its mini program that helps users find bikes nearby. Scanning the QR code on the bike unlocks it. Mobike conducted a 30-day free ride campaign when the promotion launched so users could share free rides with their WeChat friends.

10.2 WeChat Pay for Brands and Vendors

Brands and vendors can use their WeChat Pay account for online and offline transactions. Especially for offline transactions, payments are usually made by scanning QR codes provided by vendors. This novel payment method is quick and simple for both parties and has revolutionized consumer interactions in China.

Below are five major features of WeChat Pay for brands and vendors as used in China:

WeChat Pay Vendor Functions

1.   In-App Web-based Payments (公众号支付)

If brands or vendors broadcast product messages to their followers via their official WeChat account, with WeChat Pay enabled, their followers can purchase the products on the brand's WeChat store page.

When users purchase directly within WeChat, such as ordering food delivery or booking a movie ticket, they can complete the transaction without leaving WeChat. In-App web-based payments are suitable for payments within official accounts, on Moments pages and on chat pages.

Users confirm the payment amount, put in their password or use fingerprint recognition. Then can pay with their wallet balance or from their linked bank account. They receive a payment notification, are directed back to the vendor's page and receive more detailed payment information later.

This function is only available for service accounts, corporate accounts and government/media subscription accounts.

2.   In-App Payments (APP支付)

Vendors can use WeChat Pay's software development kit (SDK) to integrate WeChat Pay into their apps. For example, if users make a purchase on an external e-commerce platform app on their mobile device, they can choose to pay via WeChat on the payment page. WeChat processes the payment and returns the user to the previous app.

3. QR Code Payments (扫码支付)

Vendors can create QR codes for different items. After users scan these codes, they can see product information and payment options on their phone.

QR code payments can also be used for payments on laptop or desktop sites. After being directed to the payment page and choosing to pay via WeChat, the merchant will generate a special QR code for users to scan to pay.

This function is only available for service accounts, corporate accounts and government/media subscription accounts.

4. Quick Pay (刷卡支付)

Vendors scan the payment code shown by customers on the Quick Pay page to finish transactions quickly.

For example, in offline stores, users show the payment code - a bar code as well as a QR code - in their WeChat Wallet for vendors to scan. The payment is processed automatically. Quick Pay is suitable for offline vendors like supermarkets and convenience stores where the payment is processed face to face with customers.

Users can choose whether they want to pay with the balance in their wallet or directly from their bank account.

5. Weixin Checkout (微信买单)

WeChat helps vendors generate QR codes. Then they can print the QR code and place it in their stores. This allows users to scan it to pay when purchasing. Weixin Checkout is suitable for vendors who don't have programming and development skills.

After scanning the QR code, users confirm the amount with the vendor and input it in the interface. Then they confirm and finish the payment. The vendor later receives a message with payment details.

The "Follow After Payment" Feature

WeChat Pay can be used to direct a vendor's offline traffic to their official account with the "Follow After Payment" setting. However, it's not automatic and the settings for different payment types are different.

This feature is the default setting for Quick Pay. For in-app web-based payment and QR code payment, this setting can only be activated when the payment is above 5 RMB (0.80 USD) and it's only available to well-known brands if the In-App Payment method is being used.

Subscription accounts can't access the "Follow after payment" default setting and for service accounts with more than 500,000 followers, the system lets users opt in.

Commission Charges

Note that WeChat Pay merchants are charged a commission that varies from industry to industry but most are charged 0.6%.

10.3 E-commerce on WeChat

1. WeChat Stores

Given the growing e-commerce market in China, WeChat wanted to offer a convenient way to sell by allowing account holders to create online stores within the app.

After brands create a store on WeChat, they can link it to the menu of their official account. To buy a product, users can click the custom menu linked to the store to view and choose products and can use WeChat Pay.

The whole purchasing process can be done within WeChat so conversion rates increase. Vendors can attract customers with discounts and special offers on WeChat Store purchases.

> *A WeChat e-commerce presence is becoming the norm for all brands. However, it's particularly useful for brands that don't have a presence yet in China as WeChat enables selling cross-border through WeChat payments."*
>
> —Thomas Graziani, Co-founder of WalktheChat

Types of Online Stores on WeChat

There are four types of stores available on WeChat.

1.   **Official WeChat Stores (微信小店)** – Verified service accounts with WeChat Pay accounts can create these stores on their account management page for free.

2. **Stores hosted by a third-party** – There are service providers that allow integration within WeChat. Users build their store on these platforms and later link it to their official account. Most subscription account holders leverage these platforms to build their online stores as the official store function is not open to them. You can usually build the online store for free but these platforms usually charge a deposit or management fees. Some well-known third-party platforms include Weidian (微店, also known as Wei-Store), Weimob (微盟), Youzan (有赞), and WalktheChat.

3.   **Stores on external e-commerce platforms** – These include stores on mainstream platforms like JD.com. Note that Taobao and Tmall stores

can't be integrated into WeChat as they belong to Alibaba, Tencent's main rival. A brand can link to its own official e-commerce platform but the major drawback is that it takes a lot more time, effort and money to build and maintain.

4. Mini program online stores – With the emergence of mini programs, brands now have another option to build their online stores. The WeChat Shop Mini Program is available on the account management page to all official accounts. Advantages include simple procedures, low development costs, perfect integration with WeChat Pay and access to the "Cards and Offers" function. Since mini programs are a built-in function in WeChat, stable traffic can be ensured.

These can all be linked to official accounts. Brands can broadcast articles with sales information and launch campaigns encouraging users to visit their stores. Customers can also pay with WeChat, smoothing the conversion of traffic into sales.

> *People tend to think that it is not possible for companies outside China to create WeChat stores. It is! However, WeChat stores don't get organic traffic. They need to be promoted. WeChat stores can make huge sales. A lot of key opinion leader stores exceed 100M USD per year."*
>
> —Thomas Graziani, Co-founder of WalktheChat

Cooperating with Distributors or KOLs

Normally, brands can launch their online stores to sell their products directly. Alternatively, they can cooperate with distributors and KOLs who have their own stores on WeChat. Brands can offer special products for sale or launch flash sales campaigns on their stores.

> *Sales on WeChat are heavily supported by social proof and key opinion leaders. We found that stores in the fashion and cosmetics space were particularly successful as there is a wide choice of key opinion leaders to work with in these domains."*
>
> —Thomas Graziani, Co-founder of WalktheChat

2. Cards & Offers

WeChat also has a "Cards & Offers (卡券)" function that allows brands and vendors in specific industries with verified official accounts to distribute cards and coupons to their customers. This includes membership cards, prepaid cards, coupons and vouchers. They can be distributed by instant message, articles, custom menus, automatic messages, H5 pages, third-party apps, offline QR codes as well as WeChat Shake.

Users can keep their cards in the "Cards & Offers" section after collecting them on their personal WeChat profile page on WeChat. They can use them when they purchase online or offline and receive a notification before unused coupons expire. Some cards and coupons can also be shared with friends, creating viral spread potential.

This feature plays an indispensable supporting role in the e-commerce ecosystem within WeChat together with WeChat Pay and WeChat stores.

10.4 WeChat Brand Zone

In December 2017, WeChat launched Brand Zone as a new search function feature. Some international luxury brands, such as Cartier, Gucci, Louis Vuitton, Longchamp and Michael Kors have already made use of it.

Users can go to the "Discover" section, click "Search" and put a brand name as the search keyword. At the top of the search results is the Brand Zone. There are usually 2 tabs. The top tab is connected to an online store and also showcases the brand's latest collection. The second tab usually goes to the brand's official account. This feature allows brands to get extra exposure from organic search, drive traffic from one section to another, as well as monetize the boutique stores.

WeChat Pay is extremely popular and widely used in China. People can now easily pay bills, buy groceries or shop online using their WeChat Wallet. This ever-growing dependence signals a great opportunity and an urgent need for change. Both offline merchants and online retailers need to enable consumers to pay with WeChat and also to adapt to a changing marketing landscape based on WeChat as a social platform.

CHAPTER 11

How to Do Your CRM with WeChat

WeChat, which enables brands and companies to directly communicate through official accounts, can be used as an effective CRM (customer relationship management) tool. It can be used as a channel for brands and customers to communicate and is a powerful platform to collect customer data and analyze users' preferences.

> *Brands need to approach WeChat from a CRM perspective and service innovation perspective otherwise their WeChat account won't be anything more than a spam box."*
>
> —Thomas Meyer, Co-founder of Mobile Now Group

There are plenty of third-party CRM tools that offer all kinds of advanced functions. Integrated with those systems, such as WeChat Now, Weixinhost (侯斯特), Drip (水滴), Parllay (烽火台), Capillary and

MikeCRM (麦客), WeChat can help brands and vendors manage inquiries from users and provide more customized services. These third-party CRM tools can provide services including but not limited to the following categories:

Chatbots and MCS (Multi-Customer Solutions)

Some CRM service providers can integrate their AI-based chatbot systems in official accounts. These systems can identify what the writer is asking for quickly and give answers based on keywords in the text. When the questions are more complex, the system can guide the user to webpages with related information. With this kind of software, vendors don't need many people to deal with customer questions.

Alternatively, more personalized service can be provided by a multi-customer solutions (MCS) tool. It allows several staff members to talk to different users at the same time, so that users don't have to wait long to get their questions answered.

Database Building

Third-party CRM tools can design simple forms and surveys in order to get personal information and preferences from your customers. During a campaign, participants can be asked to fill in their personal information before getting a free gift, making a booking for a test drive or viewing an apartment.

Loyalty Programs

Loyalty programs are the most common type of CRM service. An integrated loyalty program allows users to sign up for memberships, accumulate credit, collect coupons, get discounts and enjoy other members-only privileges. These programs are widely used by hotels, food and beverage brands and retailers.

Most brands will want to map their WeChat followers to a CRM system that they own.

Firstly, the method WeChat uses to uniquely identify users doesn't allow brands to identify who that user is outside of WeChat. This need to bind a user's OpenID to an email address or mobile phone is generally the starting point for moving CRM off of WeChat.

Secondly, each WeChat user is limited to a maximum of five tags and your account is limited to 100 unique tags. If you want any scalable way to manipulate tags, it's not the WeChat backend. Once you've done a good job tagging your followers, the primary value is for targeted outbound marketing segmentation, which requires a third-party from the start."

—Thomas Meyer, Co-founder of Mobile Now Group

Other Advanced Functions

There's a lot more that CRM tools can do for brands. For e-commerce, users can order food using an online delivery brand's official account. For hotels, customers can check out the available dates and make a booking in advance.

Location-based services can also be enabled. For example, users can share their current location with an official account and receive recommendations for nearby stores or e-map navigation guides.

There are lots of options to manage customer relationships in addition to

> *Having social CRM in place in China will help you understand your followers much better and know the quality of your fans and their digital trail. This will help you provide better and more personalized content and service. Moreover, you will be able to calculate your ROI more accurately with your SCRM.*"
>
> —Sheng Pang, CEO of Juplus Digital

basic monitoring and interactions. Rather than passively responding to customers, make good use of powerful third-party tools to collect the data that you need and use it to better understand your customers.

Customers demand open conversations and timely communication with brands, but that is not everything. Enhancing your services and products should be a key goal, especially when there are great tools that can help you understand what your customers need.

> *There is no 'one solution fits it all', which is why customizable and integration-friendly CRM solutions are the way to go.*"
>
> —Thomas Meyer, Co-founder of Mobile Now Group

CHAPTER 12

How to Use WeChat Mini Programs for Business

WeChat has evolved from an instant messaging app into a comprehensive platform that includes an e-commerce ecosystem. But it's not finished. Tencent has indicated that it will continue to develop and extend the app and that they're committed to making it the only platform that people will need.

One way that WeChat is working to achieve this goal is with mini programs, their apps within the app. In the year since they were introduced in 2017, over 580,000 mini programs have been developed and 170 million monthly users have made use of them. They cover over 20 industries and more than 200 sub-categories and international brands like KFC, Coach and Tesla have released mini programs.

Beware that they're changing rapidly so the information here will quickly be out of date but they are the future of WeChat so it's important to understand them.

12.1 Overview of Mini Programs

When Tencent officially launched the mini program platform, it was considered a milestone for WeChat and a turning point for mobile operating systems. Industry insiders even predict that WeChat will one day rival iOS and Android as another major mobile operating system.

Mini programs are the embedded cloud-based applications that operate within the WeChat system. However, the term "app" is avoided to differentiate them from Apple and Android products. Users can find them by searching with keywords, scanning special mini program codes, clicking links embedded in WeChat articles or through mini program cards.

Using them means there's no need to install lots of apps, saving phone storage and optimizing the user experience. Although they're more limited than full function apps, for brands they are much more. They can be used to nurture a virtual community, launch creative campaigns, build an e-commerce platform and promote their brick-and-mortar stores.

They're much easier to develop than a more complex app and can be used to test market viability and gather feedback without a large investment. Their sharing features and huge user base ensure considerable usage.

12.2 Using Mini Programs

Getting Access to Mini Programs

For new users, there's no mini program page or button. You have to start using a mini program to activate them on the "Discovery" page. There are several ways to find them to use them for the first time.

You can use WeChat's search bar or get one from a friend or group via chat. If an official account links to a mini program, subscribers receive a notification and can access it by clicking on the message or by clicking on it on the official account's profile page. Users can also access them by clicking mini program cards in WeChat articles.

Mini program codes are a bit special. They use an exclusive, independent QR code format that can only be created on WeChat, ensuring control and keeping them within their ecosystem. The codes can be posted on WeChat Moments or sent to friends. They can be opened by long pressing the code or by scanning it.

How Mini Programs Are Being Used

In less than a year, mini programs have accumulated a stable user base and growing popularity. They can replace a large selection of lightly used apps or be used as light versions of current apps. They can also be used as trial versions of full apps and lead to downloads. There are four major ways that mini programs are used at the moment:

Anything we say and write about mini programs will be quickly out of date. Even by China standards the format is changing incredibly fast. It's also clear that the direction of the format is in evolution. Tencent is a very adaptive company and China's mobile ecosystem is in state of constant dynamic flux. Even the WeChat team themselves can't predict with 100% confidence where things will be in a year's time."

—Matthew Brennan, Co-founder of China Channel

Daily necessity tools

Practical mini programs are the most popular type and cover most daily needs such as transportation, time management, translation and polls. For example, users can use different mini programs to book tickets and check bus and train schedules.

Information and entertainment

Mini programs can help users to access useful information such as exchange rates. For entertainment-related services, users can check film reviews and purchase movie tickets directly on mini programs. There are also plenty of mini program games.

E-commerce

Brands now have the option of building their e-commerce platform using a mini program. This brings low development costs and perfect integration with WeChat Pay and the "Cards & Offers" function. Since mini programs are a built-in function in WeChat, stable traffic can also be ensured.

Mini programs can also be used to launch giveaways, special offers as well as UGC (user-generated content) collection campaigns to help boost sales or increase brand awareness.

As WeChat gradually allows developers to add multimedia content in their mini programs, and given the popularity of live streaming in China, some vendors have even started doing live streaming on mini programs to boost sales. For example, Mogujie (蘑菇街), a social commerce app for fashion, launched their own mini program that allows sellers to host live streams and sell.

In this mini program, sellers launch live streams to showcase the clothes and accessories they sell. If viewers are interested, they can select the items on the left, make an order and finish payment within the mini program, giving it a "See Now, Buy Now" feature. Flash sales campaigns can also be launched.

WeChat-related services

Mini programs also offer convenience for those who work closely with official accounts. For example, the "Official Account Assistant (公众平台助手)" mini program shows the latest account statistics and followers' comments. This reduces the need to constantly log in to the desktop version. The "Weixin Checkout (微信买单)" mini program allows vendors to consult and manage transaction details easily.

"WeChat Index (微信指数)" also has its own mini program. It measures the popularity of designated keywords based on their search volume, their appearance in articles and their appearance in shared articles on users' Moments pages. Users can input a keyword and track its popularity in the last 7, 30 or 90 days.

This index is an important indicator for brands and social media managers because of the platform's huge base of prime demographic users. It can help brands identify trends and decide whether to incorporate them in their social media content, while also revealing the popularity of a brand or an official account.

12.3 Mini Programs as an O2O Facilitator

In order to encourage more people to use mini programs, lots of new features have been added. We'll go into detail about two special features designed to help brands and vendors promote their brick-and-mortar stores and work as O2O facilitators.

> *Currently e-commerce is by far the hottest category of mini program. WeChat's team have worked to produce a framework so brands can easily create e-commerce stores which replicate the kind of experience which Chinese internet users are comfortable and familiar with from years of using Taobao and Tmall. They have streamlined the checkout process and supercharged mini programs in a variety of ways that, when added together, mean that conversion is easier through mini programs than normal web page stores."*
>
> —Matthew Brennan, Co-founder of China Channel

Store Mini Programs (门店小程序)

In April 2017, WeChat launched a new feature called the "Store Mini Program" which shows users basic information about an offline store, like a virtual business card.

Firstly, despite its name, it's not currently a mini program but a feature related to mini programs. With this feature, brands and vendors with official accounts can set up a store mini program quickly using their account management page without further programming. Basic store information, including the store name, address, opening hours, contact phone number and store photos, are displayed. It's a good idea to upload photos of the latest products and campaign posters to give customers a quick and clear product reference.

Store mini programs can also distribute membership cards and one type of coupon or voucher. Branches in the same chain are considered different stores and can distribute different cards and coupons from other branches. An interface to allow customers to collect membership cards and vouchers can also be added.

In general, store mini programs are an effective online-to-offline tunnel for brands, especially when they want to boost sales in physical stores.

Mini Programs Nearby (附近的小程序)

In May 2017, WeChat released the "Mini Programs Nearby" function which allows brands with offline locations to display their mini programs. When users are near the brand's location, mini programs for nearby businesses show up there. It helps merchants to reach their potential customers more easily.

This function plays a significant role in connecting online customers with offline stores. It puts practical brand information into customers' pockets, increasing brand awareness, traffic and sales.

Imagine this scene: A customer is in a large shopping mall. She stops and takes out her smartphone to check where she can buy a luxury bag. Instead of launching a map, she opens WeChat and goes directly to the "Mini Programs Nearby" section. Before she decides which store to visit, she can look through all the mini programs nearby and check out the products and campaign information displayed.

12.4 The Future of Mini Programs and How They Might Reshape the Retail Industry

Mini program features provide new possibilities for brands and vendors to explore and using them effectively can lead to a win-win situation for both vendors and customers.

For brands and vendors, mini programs provide an alternative O2O conversion tunnel, connecting online users with offline physical stores. In addition, unlike offline sales where many customers leave immediately after purchasing without leaving any contact details or personal information, mini programs offer valuable user statistics that help vendors understand their customers better.

They're also a very convenient platform for customers. After users access a mini program for the first time, it stays in their mini program files until it's deleted. This makes it easy to access and saves time. It's like subscribing to an official account and is likely to increase usage rates. "Mini Programs Nearby" also increases customer convenience.

Frequent updates mean that mini programs keep improving and adding functions and they're now open to third party operators that can help brands develop their own mini programs. This lowers the barrier to entry and makes it cost-effective. There will be more and more new features and opportunities that will further reshape the retail industry in China.

CHAPTER 13

Your Next Steps on WeChat

From what we can see today the future of WeChat in the next 2 years will be in large part based around improving search and improving mini programs. For WeChat mini programs, it's no exaggeration to say that they are the future of WeChat. The only question is how much will they go on to impact the rest of the mobile ecosystem in China."

—Matthew Brennan, Co-founder of China Channel

Part II is about WeChat, its diverse functions and how Chinese consumers are living with it. It's becoming the operating system for most Chinese users and continues to add more and more diverse functions.

There's a common misconception that every brand that has entered China must have their own official WeChat account. However, this is not entirely so. For example, WeChat is not really for B2B brands. Their target audience is really niche due to their professional expertise and is less interesting for general users.

Another false assumption is that a brand can rely on WeChat alone and expect a presence there to bring them everything they want. As a semi-closed platform, WeChat maintains a relatively intimate relationship between users and also between users and brands. This means that initially, it's not the ideal platform to gain popularity and grow followers. A more reasonable approach is to leverage WeChat after you've accumulated a stable audience on other platforms, and then drive them to WeChat for further relationship development.

In Part I, three categories of brands were discussed based on their China market entry mode. They were international brands already in China, brands doing cross-border e-commerce and overseas brands serving Chinese visitors. In this chapter, we'll see how these three types of brands should use WeChat and the most relevant tools or functions for each type of brand.

1. International Brands Already in China

These brands have already set up a legal entity in China. They have online stores, brick-and-mortar stores or both in mainland China. They employ local staff and are well-adapted to the local e-commerce ecosystem. These brands are already known to some Chinese consumers.

Official Account and WeChat Articles

It's good for these brands to have their own official WeChat account. However, as mentioned above, WeChat is not for everyone. Before making the decision, brands should think about who their target audience is and whether they can leverage WeChat's functions for maximum effect.

Regular posting is essential to keep the audience updated. Articles are the most popular content type on WeChat. Most subscription accounts post one to three articles once a day while service accounts usually post four to five articles once a week.

These articles are also important for interactive campaigns. Brands can encourage users to leave a comment under an article for lucky draws, or ask them to share an article to Moments to accumulate enough "likes" to receive special offers, which helps them get more exposure.

Custom Menu Bar for CRM

WeChat is an ideal tool for customer relationship management. A great variety of third-party CRM tools can be integrated within WeChat as well. Brands can make full use of these functions to create an efficient communication channel with customers for one-on-one messages, loyalty programmes and other services. The platform also helps brands collect useful user data to build a database for analysis to understand customer needs better.

These CRM-related functions can be integrated in the custom menu bar so that users can find the right service easily when they enter the official account interface.

WeChat Stores and the "Cards & Offers" Function

WeChat is well-suited to driving sales conversions. Brands can embed links to external e-commerce platforms, with the exception of Taobao and Tmall which belong to competitor Alibaba Group. These links can be added at the end of articles so that interested readers can buy the items described in the article.

Alternatively, brands can open their own WeChat store. There are several ways to do this and it can even be done using a mini program. Users can access the store easily and use coupons and membership cards they've collected virtually.

The full compatibility of WeChat stores with the app itself also makes the whole purchasing process smooth and easy.

WeChat Pay

As Chinese consumers are accustomed to mobile payments, brands in China need to support mobile payment methods for online and brick-and-mortar stores. Given the popularity of WeChat Pay in mainland China, it's become a must to incorporate it.

Wi-Fi via WeChat

This is a special WeChat function. Brands or merchants that have brick-and-mortar stores and official accounts can activate it and only followers of the brand's official account can use it. It allows these users to access free Wi-Fi through WeChat when they are at the brand's store or offices and also allows access to the merchant's online services. This attracts offline followers at zero cost while brands can get valuable user data.

2. Brands Doing Cross-Border E-Commerce

These brands offer their products via international retailers or suppliers. They haven't officially entered China yet and use an intermediary business entity or online sales outlets in China. Rather than setting up an official account on major platforms, it's more useful for them to engage KOLs for their initial promotions.

WeChat Articles on a KOL's Official Account

To help a "newcomer" brand gain recognition with Chinese consumers, it's common to pay KOLs to contribute a comprehensive article introducing the brand with product recommendations and reviews. Links to other online sales platforms or a flagship store the brand has already set up should be included in the article.

WeChat Stores and the "Cards & Offers" Function

Brands can offer specific products for sale in a KOL's WeChat store. Some KOLs' WeChat stores have a selection of overseas products for sale. Customers can purchase onsite and get product updates at the same time. Cards and offers can also be distributed to stimulate sales.

Official Accounts and WeChat Articles

After the brand has gained some customers, they can open an official account and start posting regular content for further promotion.

3. Overseas Brands Serving Chinese Visitors

These brands are physically located outside of China. Their goal is not to sell their products to consumers living in China. Instead, their objective is to attract Chinese visitors to use their services when they're abroad. They are usually brands in the hospitality industry like restaurants and hotels or schools that want to attract international students from China.

They're likely unknown to most Chinese consumers and their biggest challenge is standing out from the crowd and getting noticed by outbound visitors.

Official Account

Having an official account is a prerequisite for the features described so to benefit most, these brand must register for one. However, please remember the differences between WeChat's international version and Weixin that were mentioned in section 7.2 otherwise, you'll never reach your target audience. Outbound Chinese visitors use Weixin.

Overseas Moments Ads

Since early 2017, WeChat allowed overseas brands to launch Moments ads in specific countries or regions. Note that it's still at the open beta stage so it's not available to everyone and is only available in certain regions. This allows brands and merchants located overseas to target outbound Chinese tourists or Chinese expatriates.

Overseas Moments ads target users that have logged in to WeChat in a specific country or region. However, so far, no city-level targeting is possible.

At the time of printing, WeChat overseas advertising was open for 16 countries and regions including Hong Kong, Macau, Taiwan, Japan, Korea, Malaysia, Singapore, Thailand, the United States, Australia, Germany, France, the United Kingdom, Italy, Canada and New Zealand. The minimum budget varies by country and region, as well as the ad format.

The "Cards & Offers" Function

Overseas brands can give away digital coupons via WeChat articles or WeChat Shake. Users can turn on their phone's bluetooth then open WeChat Shake and select "Nearby". They can shake their device to get coupons, vouchers or other special offers from nearby merchants. Coupons should have wide validity dates so that users can collect them before a trip to use later overseas. It's a great way to drive traffic to offline merchants, especially retail stores and restaurants.

WeChat Pay

WeChat Pay is expanding to a number of overseas regions and countries. With the number of outbound Chinese tourists increasing, it's become a rigid demand for overseas merchants to support Chinese digital payment methods in order to satisfy their needs, offer convenience and encourage them to spend more. WeChat Pay accounts can now be linked to foreign credit cards in Hong Kong, Macao and Taiwan and this can also be done by foreigners living in mainland China.

The major advantage of enabling WeChat Pay is that outbound Chinese visitors make purchases overseas in RMB. Local currency is converted into RMB based on real-time exchange rates while WeChat Pay settles each transaction with overseas vendors based on the price in local currency. For unsupported currencies, transactions can be made in USD. Currently, major currencies include, but are not limited to, GBP, HKD, USD, JPY, CAD, AUD, EUR, NZD, KRW.

PART III

Weibo: China's Online Hotspot

CHAPTER 14

What is Weibo?

Officially launched in 2009, Sina Weibo* is the leading microblogging and social networking site in China and another must for marketers. Weibo's Q3 2017 financial report states that it has about 376 million monthly active users and over 165 million daily active users.

Weibo is an open platform for microblogging and social networking. It was developed for users to follow celebrities and share user-generated content (UGC). Weibo is the most dominant source of news and gossip and people are there mainly to stay up to date, share and comment.

Weibo is often called the Chinese version of Twitter but it's really more like a combination of Twitter and Facebook with additional unique features. Users can make their own posts and interact with other people's posts by liking, commenting and reposting. There used to be a word limit of 140 characters per post. In January, 2016, the limit was removed for original posts but still applies to comments and reposts. In every post, users can insert various rich media such as images, videos, music, emoticons and polls without plugins.

* Note: In this book, Weibo refers to Sina Weibo.

14.1 Weibo: A Day in the Life

Li Min is 24. She's a marketing manager in Guangzhou. It's a sunny Monday. She's having breakfast when she opens Weibo on her phone to post a picture of her breakfast in her Friend Circle. Then she scrolls down to check the latest posts. She likes some interesting ones and reposts some to her page. After a while, she receives likes and some comments from her friends. What a great start to the day!

During work, she manages her company's official Weibo page. She checks the "Hot Search" and "Hot Post" ranking for inspiration for the day's post. She sees that a recently released movie is a big topic on Weibo so she asks her team to draft a post about it. She follows an actress from a new show that she really likes. She also replies to comments on three posts that her team posted yesterday.

After work, she goes to yoga class. She wants to share her progress with her friends so she uses Weibo Story to record and publish a series of short videos showing her new moves.

Li Min is interested in skin care and makeup. While she's having dinner, she opens Weibo and clicks on posts by a group of makeup KOLs she follows to see what they've posted today. One of her favorite bloggers is live streaming her skin care routine. She watches it while finishing her meal.

Before going to bed, Li Min checks the "Hot Search" and "Hot Post" ranking again to see if she missed any important news or entertainment gossip. She notices a direct message from one of the beauty bloggers she follows and is pleasantly surprised to find that she's won a hair dryer because she reposted a lucky draw post. As Li Min doesn't need another hair dryer, the blogger agrees to pay her the cash equivalent using Weibo Wallet. This has literally made her day. Li Min goes to sleep happy.

14.2 Weibo for Social Networking

As a social networking app, Weibo's basic function is to display short posts like Twitter. Posts can include text, pictures, articles, video via Miaopai, live streams via Yizhibo and external links, etc. Users can follow others, repost, comment and like posts. While updates and comments are public, messages are private.

Friend Circle

Friend Circle (好友圈) is a group for users who follow each other. If users post to Friend Circle, it can only be seen by members.

Live Streaming

Weibo live streaming is supported by Yizhibo, an interactive entertainment app. Users can make and watch live streams and communicate with others in real time. When watching live streams, audiences can grab red packets, which are virtual red envelopes worth money, make comments and send gifts to the broadcasters. Live streamers can add topics and their location to find other broadcasters in the same city, which helps to build a local e-community. Live streaming enhances the interactivity between broadcasters and their followers.

Weibo Window

Weibo Window is a product display platform for Weibo users. Users add information, pictures and external e-commerce links - only available for Taobao and Jumei - for the product. Customers can browse and buy it on the e-commerce platform.

Weibo Wallet

Weibo Wallet is a payment function that was launched in 2012. All users with a Weibo account have access to this function, and they can link their Weibo Wallet with an Alipay account for top ups and withdrawals. Meanwhile, users can also connect their Weibo Wallet with Taobao accounts for payment.

The popularity of Weibo Wallet is much lower than its rival WeChat Pay and it's not a common option for B2C payments. It's mostly used for purchasing Weibo VIP memberships. Other functions include money transfers through red packets, mobile data top ups, utility bill payments and charity donations.

Weibo Story

Weibo officially launched Weibo Story on April 19th, 2017. It's like Instagram Stories or Facebook Stories. Users can easily post a 15-second short video or photo to quickly share moments from their day. When they share multiple videos or photos, they appear together in a slideshow format. It has additional features such as stickers, text effects, filters and editing functions. The post can't be reposted, downloaded or shared to external platforms and disappears after 24 hours.

14.3 User Demographics

Here are some key facts about Weibo users. The majority of Weibo's monthly active users are Gen Y and under 30. They make up 80% of the total monthly active users. There are more male users than female users, 56.3% to 43.7%, and among monthly active users, half are from third and fourth tier cities. This resonates with Weibo's goal of becoming the national social platform in China. 92% of their monthly active users access Weibo via its mobile app. They are most interested in entertainment related topics, such as celebrities, comics, literature, movies, dining out, sports etc. Each user on average follows around 200 official accounts and one new post appears in their stream every five minutes. The majority of Weibo users are well-educated. 77.8% have a bachelor's degree or above.

14.4 Development of Sina Weibo

The Weibo War

Back in 2010, there were multiple microblogging platforms in China offered by Sina, Sohu, NetEase and Tencent. During that time, Sina Weibo and Tencent Weibo were the two microblogging giants that dominated the market from the start.

Sina was the first to introduce a microblogging service in China. With its first-mover advantage, it was able to get lots of celebrities to open accounts on the platform, enabling it to amass a considerable user base in just one year.

Tencent opened its own microblogging site called Tencent Weibo a year later, as a defense against Sina. It caught up quickly in the following years, especially after users were able to log onto the service using their QQ and WeChat accounts.

By 2012, Tencent Weibo had a user base of 540 million with 87 million daily active users, surpassing Sina Weibo's 503 million user base and 46.2 million active users.

Yet, Tencent in its 2012 annual report revealed that the growth of Tencent Weibo users in China was decelerating. The major reasons includes the platform failing to capture users' interests in gossip as well as internal competition with Qzone, in terms of traffic. In July 2014, Tencent announced that it would discontinue Tencent Weibo, so that the group could allocate resources to more important pillar products, namely WeChat.

The Death and Revival of Weibo

Sina Weibo has achieved explosive popularity in China since it was launched. However, it began losing momentum in 2012, and discussions began about the death of Weibo. Social analysts have pointed out various causes for their slowdown but the main reasons were the government's media crackdown and the rise of WeChat.

Since Xi Jinping took power in 2012, the government has increased its control and censorship of mass media. Since Weibo is a platform for people to publicize and express their opinions, interest and debate around controversial events can spread quickly. The government has introduced measures to tamp down online debate and increase control of microblogging by requiring real-name registration and launching anti-rumor campaigns. People were concerned about freedom of speech online and started deserting Weibo.

On top of that, WeChat was launched in 2011 and expanded rapidly to over 200 million users in 2 years. Many Weibo users began to spend more time on WeChat in the years following its launch. WeChat has a more closed setup and its messaging and social networking functions provided another platform for people to connect and interact. Weibo experienced a 40% decline in active users from Q2 to Q4 2012 and there was also a significant drop of 56 million registered accounts in 2014.

But Weibo is much more today than what it was then. Sina took several approaches to rebuild its user base. For example, it began to tap into users in lower tier cities and younger age groups through its pre-installed app starting in 2013. Weibo also initiated a campaign in 2014 to sponsor bloggers to create content.

But more than this, the huge popularity of short videos and live streaming have played a major role in Weibo's renaissance. Weibo partnered with video sharing app Miaopai back in 2013 and the live streaming app Yizhibo in 2016. Users can now access them on Weibo. Many web celebrities have relocated to Weibo because of this and their fans are following them to the platform. Because of this, Morgan Stanley predicts that Weibo will see monthly active users rise to 400 million by 2018.

CHAPTER 15

Weibo's Working Model

Weibo is a discussion platform to talk about the latest news, celebrity gossip and personal interests and is one of the most popular social media platforms in China. It has a simple working model with entertainment at its heart.

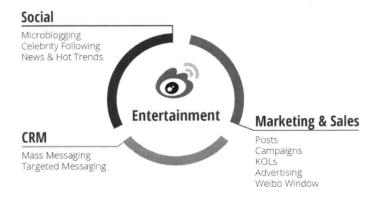

Weibo's Working Model

Social
Microblogging
Celebrity Following
News & Hot Trends

Entertainment

Marketing & Sales
Posts
Campaigns
KOLs
Advertising
Weibo Window

CRM
Mass Messaging
Targeted Messaging

15.1   How Does Weibo Work?

Social Networking

In 2009, before WeChat was launched, Weibo's first batch of users primarily updated their status and connected with friends on the platform. Users became addicted and this phase lasted for some time. Then, more and more celebrities and media outlets opened accounts and lots of people started following these big names, boosting the platform.

After this phase users started to leverage Weibo for self-broadcasting. They wrote posts or uploaded photos that they thought would reflect their unique personality. They were willing to tag themselves as bloggers in different domains and connect with people who had similar interests for recognition and a sense of belonging.

The beautiful, professional, knowledgeable, odd and funny in this crowded scene began to stand out and gradually, certain personalities became well-known. Those with the foresight and ambition to use this open platform to create or increase their own fame won in the end and this expanded Weibo's scope beyond being merely a social networking site.

Marketing and Advertising

Because Weibo is an open, public platform, it's a brand favourite for digital promotion. Once qualified brands and merchants register their official account, they can launch all kinds of marketing campaigns as well as paid advertising.

Topic hashtags, the search function and feed recommendations help brands reach potential users with their campaign posts. It's much easier to gain popularity and accumulate followers on Weibo than it is on WeChat.

In addition to campaigns and traditional advertising, brands use brand ambassadors and paid placements with Weibo personalities to gain attention. These well-known influencers are referred to as KOLs in China - Key Opinion Leaders. Formal agreements are entered into with KOLs who are compensated monetarily. Unlike the West, it's still not a requirement on most platforms for the KOL to declare these arrangements or to clearly label sponsored content. Many brands prefer this kind of promotion as it's less expensive, reaches a wider audience and generally has a higher conversion rate.

Sales

To facilitate sales on the platform, they cooperate with Taobao and Tmall to launch the Weibo Window function for direct sales. The driving force behind the cooperation is that Alibaba Group, which owns Taobao and Tmall, became a Weibo shareholder in April 2013. At that time, Alibaba Group held an 18% stake in Weibo which rose to 31% by the end of March 2017.

With Weibo Window, both individual sellers on Taobao and brands that have their official store on Tmall can import product links from the two platforms and sell without switching between platforms.

The platform also has the Weibo Wallet function that allows users to buy and sell directly on Weibo. They can also manage all their items and purchasing orders on Weibo and link their Alipay account to top up their mobile phone data, pay utility bills, send red packets, purchase directly on the platform, etc. However, its popularity is far lower than WeChat Wallet.

CRM

Weibo can also be used for customer relationship management (CRM). The platform provides basic customer service functions like mass messaging and custom menu bars in the private message dialog box. Users can also get information by sending direct messages to a brand's account or by using the keyword auto-reply function in the menu bar.

It's important to use these standard features to keep a communication channel open with customers.

15.2   The Heart of Weibo: Entertainment

China's Online Hotspot

Weibo is an information-driven platform. Information on Weibo spreads quickly, efficiently and widely. Users get the latest news and information here, and then voice their own opinions and start discussions with other netizens. They talk about celebrity gossip, movies and TV dramas, current events and other personal interests.

Sometimes heated discussions over an incident become hot topics on Weibo. To earn additional exposure, brands often integrate positive or funny trending issues in their copywriting.

Weibo users now prefer multimedia content. Short videos have become the most popular content type on Weibo. Weibo Story, which posts 15-second short videos or photos in a slideshow format, has seen remarkable growth in active users. Users also like to watch all kinds of live streaming on Weibo, like brand special events, celebrity interviews and Wanghong broadcasts.

The heart of Weibo is entertainment. Most users come to Weibo for funny, interesting multimedia content. This makes it a great platform for brands to show their unique personality and win loyal followers.

CHAPTER 16

How to Market on Weibo

With such a vast audience and high penetration, Weibo is one of the most effective marketing channels for businesses to engage with potential customers in China. However, building a quality Weibo account is definitely not an easy task. It requires a lot of time, effort and, more importantly, good marketing strategies.

16.1 Weibo Accounts

To start marketing, you need a Weibo account. There are 2 types of regular accounts on Weibo - personal and corporate. A personal account is for individual users while the corporate account is for corporates, media, and organizations. There is no registration fee for setting up these two types of regular accounts.

Once you have a regular corporate account, take the necessary steps to get it verified. Verified accounts, indicated by an orange or blue 'V', have extra marketing features and privileges and clearly indicate that they're legitimate to the audience. Personal and corporate accounts have different verification procedures.

Personal Accounts

Verifying a personal account for someone in mainland China is relatively simple. You need a local mobile phone number to connect to the account and a profile photo of your face. Only relatively active accounts with more than 100 followers that follow more than 30 accounts can be verified. You're also required to have at least 2 friends with verified personal accounts.

If you're not in China and you'd like to have a verified personal account, you need to provide more documentation, including copies of your proof of employment, a business card, proof of identity, such as your passport or driver's license, and certification in any industry relevant to your account.

Corporate Accounts

To verify the corporate account of a China registered company, you need to submit your Chinese business license, an application letter and the contact details of the account administrator. You will also need to pay a certification fee of 300 RMB.

However, if your company is outside China, you'll need to submit your company registration documents with a certified Chinese translation, an application letter, a third-party authorization letter, the account administrator's contact details and a verification fee of 1,000 USD.

For overseas account verification, you can either submit the documents by yourself or you can hire an agency to prepare all the necessary documents.

Once the account is verified, an orange 'V' is displayed next to the profile picture for verified personal accounts and a blue 'V' is shown on verified corporate accounts. Both types of verified accounts have access to the Activity Center to launch campaigns. Verified corporate accounts can also pin posts, change their cover image and add up to 5 images in the slideshow region.

With a verified official account, you can then kickstart your marketing activities on Weibo.

16.2 Posting Frequency

Weibo is a content-heavy platform that is designed to expedite the spread of information. Every day, there are about 100 million messages posted on Weibo. With such intense competition, posting frequency is very important. To get your followers' attention and let them remember you, you have to post more and need to post on a regular schedule in order to keep the account consistent.

It's common for official accounts to publish at least one post per day. Some larger brands, especially those in retail and FMCG, usually have a higher posting frequency of 3-5 posts per day. Some Weibo bloggers even broadcast to their audience every few hours. If you have just set up a new Weibo account, two or three posts per day is highly recommended to accumulate some initial content for visitors.

16.3 Content Types

International brands often make their accounts look very much like a commercial by constantly posting beautiful pictures of their products. However, Weibo is where people look for entertainment and engagement. To keep followers engaged, content needs to be diversified with a mix of informing, interacting, entertaining and promoting. It also needs to show an understanding of current styles and trending topics. Positioning should transmit meaningful values and knowledge to the readers.

When you're working out your content plan, here are some content categories that are recommended.

Practical Tips

Practical tips are a popular type of content on Weibo and they usually have high engagement and tend to be shared more often. You can create informative posts that educate the consumer on specific topics that are related to your industry. Sometimes, you can also give instructions on how to make the best use of your products for soft promotion.

Hot Topics

Hot topics can be related to anything - a recent film or TV series, celebrities, books, catchwords, special occasions and more. Recent hot topics and hashtags can be easily found on the Weibo search page. However, these issues change rapidly from hour to hour so you need to stay tuned. Whenever you spot a popular subject related to your product or industry that's being heavily discussed on Weibo, seize the opportunity and create a post about it right away.

Funny Posts

Adding humor to your posts is a great way to catch the audience's attention. A witty post with a joke or a funny meme appeals to your audience's positive emotions and helps them to remember you. Sometimes you can also poke fun at yourself by doing a parody of your company or your industry. This approach might be less effective for highly regulated industries, such as healthcare and finance.

Interactive Posts

Pairing social media with interactive content is a great way to drive engagement and trigger discussion. You can interact with your followers by asking questions, inviting them to participate in discussions or polls, collecting their opinions on a specific topic, etc. However, this kind of interactive content should be posted only after the account has a following or there won't be much interaction.

Brand-Related

You can talk about your brand, team, achievements and, most importantly, your products and their unique features. You can also update your followers on recent product developments or events. Sharing user reviews, media coverage or news features is a great way to showcase credibility.

Sales

Showcasing products is a great way to increase visibility and sales conversions. Whenever there's a special offer, make an announcement on Weibo to notify your followers. When there's a new product launch, you can show sneak peeks to build anticipation. Meanwhile, you can give away some exclusive trial products to your followers to collect feedback and generate buzz and excitement about the launch.

Tips

• Topical and funny posts can be very successful when they're closely related to a trending topic, your brand and/or your target consumers.

• Content types can be mixed wisely to achieve the synergy. For example, sales promotion posts must be fun or interactive to engage followers.

• Ask your staff to share on Weibo. It's common for employees to promote their company's products.

• Post frequency for established brands is about 3-8 times a day, especially in retail.

• You need to use videos and GIFs and should try to live stream about once a week.

16.4 Making Posts Pop with Visuals

Visuals are crucial to catch a reader's attention. Whenever possible, add rich media such as images, videos and emoticons to your posts.

Images

A Weibo post can accommodate up to 9 pictures. If you have enough visual material or an in-house designer, try to use 9 pictures at once. They'll be displayed in a nice 3x3 grid and create an eye-catching effect. A combination of 3, 4, or 6 images also display nicely on both desktop and mobile interfaces.

GIFs

GIFs are animated images that are popular on social media as they offer a clear, wordless and often funny way to express a reaction, tell a story or communicate a joke. GIFs can also be used effectively for product introductions. Rather than overwhelming readers with text, you can describe your product's features and demonstrate them with a collection of GIFs.

Biaoqingbao

Biaoqing, is a meme type common on the internet in China that combines an image and a catchphrase. The images are usually a photoshopped blend of photos and crude illustrations. Most of them are just for fun, while some have a deeper meaning to them. If you want to localize your messages, you can incorporate biaoqing into posts but it's important to understand the meaning of these memes before trying to use them.

Videos

Videos can be uploaded to Weibo directly or reposted from other websites and apps. Weibo supports major video formats and allows URLs from many other video sites including Sina Broadcast, Youku, Tudou, Ku6, Sohu, 56, iQiyi, Phoenix, Yinyuetai and LeTV.

Tip

- Use Weibo's catchy emojis, do live streaming at least once a week, and use GIFs to make your posts stand out.

16.5 Other Features That Can Make Content Stand Out

Long Articles

Sometimes you may need to create an in-depth post to share information, in this case you can use the "Long Article"(长 微博) function. It has a similar layout to a WeChat or LinkedIn article. Aside from core text, you can also insert images, video and music to make the article more informative and engaging.

These articles include a 'Tipping' feature. Before you push a long article, you can choose to put it on or off. If it's on, other readers can tip you if they like your article.

Hashtags

With hashtags, users can easily track a topic on Weibo and monitor discussions related to it. The platform uses a double hashtag format so they look like #this# or #这个# instead of #this or #这个.

When you click a hashtag, it takes you to a page of statistics that shows the number of views, shares and followers for it. You can also view all the posts with the same hashtag and can easily tell whether a hashtag is popular or not. Picking a relevant hot topic and engaging in the discussion is a great way to drive engagement and build account followership.

There's another unique function referred to as "owning a hashtag". You can apply to become the "topic host" of a specific hashtag. If you're the topic host, you can edit the hashtag landing page and invite relevant accounts to join the community. You can also monitor the flow of content and pin posts. It's a good way to promote your account and content, especially if the topic is popular. However, the topic host is required to stay active and make more than one post per week. If not, they will no longer be the host and other accounts can apply to host it.

16.6 Weibo Campaigns

Launching campaigns is an important part of Weibo marketing. Not only can they bring you new followers but also keep your existing followers engaged. In general, Weibo users love participating in all sorts of campaigns for fun and to win prizes.

There are two major types of campaign on Weibo; **system campaigns** and **creative campaigns**:

- System campaigns have basic formats and rules defined by Weibo and they can only be launched by verified corporate accounts.

- Creative campaigns are created and customized according to the organizer's needs and goals. They can be launched by all accounts.

Launching a Weibo campaign is free so you only need to allocate budget for prizes and promotion.

System Campaigns

To launch a system campaign, go the Activity Center (活动中心) in the Management Center (管理中心) to set up and submit the campaign details. Once the campaign is approved, it will be launched on the scheduled day. There are 6 default types of system campaigns that Weibo offers:

Repost Campaigns (有奖转发)

This requires users to repost a designated post. As the organizer, you can also decide if users need to follow your account or tag friends in the repost message. At the end of the campaign, winners are randomly picked by the system.

Content Collection Campaigns (有奖征集)

This encourages users to contribute original content related to a certain topic. The format includes reviews, pictures, videos or slogans. At the end of the campaign, you can pick the winners based on the quality of content.

Pre-ordering Campaigns (预约购买)

This allows users to pre-order products before they're launched. At the end of the campaign, only people who have participated can purchase the product. These are a good way to draw attention and create buzz before an official release. It seems that purchase links must be connected to Alibaba properties or they will be difficult to post.

Free Trial Campaigns (免费试用)

This allows you to distribute product samples to your target audience when you launch a new product. To get the samples, users give reasons why they should be selected. At the end of the campaign, you can pick the winners based on the quality of their content. At the same time, you can collect valuable market feedback on the product.

Lucky Roulette Campaigns (幸运转盘)

This allows users to spin a roulette wheel for a chance to win a prize immediately. You can offer a wide range of prizes in this campaign.

Flash Sales Campaigns (限时抢)

This is similar to a Lucky Roulette Campaign but it's more suitable for e-commerce and O2O businesses. In a Flash Sales Campaign, users can win gifts or get special discounts for promoted products for a limited time.

Creative Campaigns

Compared to system campaigns, creative campaigns allow more room to design the format and rules. A creative campaign is usually created as a post that clearly states the participation procedures, prizes, campaign period, number of winners and other terms and conditions.

At the end of the campaign, you can either handpick the winners by yourself, or use a third-party application called 微博转发抽奖平台 to select winners who followed the campaign rules. By using this add-on, the winners will be notified automatically by private message to submit their contact details so you can send them prizes and build your customer database.

Tips

- Eye-catching visual designs, attractive incentives and easy, fun participation formats are the best ingredients for a successful Weibo campaign.

16.7 Weibo KOLs

Similar to WeChat, engaging KOLs is one of the most effective ways to promote your account and business. KOLs appear to have a stronger influence in China than they do in the West. They don't just spread information. They also promote attitudes and approaches that affect the buying decisions of their followers. In general, Chinese people trust the information they receive from KOLs more than ads or other kinds of media. By leveraging their large base of online followers, you can easily spread your message and market your product or service.

Types of KOLs on Weibo

There are five key types of Weibo KOLs:

Celebrities - This includes famous actors, singers and TV personalities. The cost for one Weibo post from celebrities like Xue Zhiqian can be over one million RMB, according to websites like MiHui.com and agencies like Louis Communication and Gushan Culture.

Wanghong (网红) or "web celebrities" - These are the Kendall Jenners of China. They include people like Zhang Dayi and comedic blogger Papi Jiang. The cost for wanghong is generally 20% to 40% lower than mainstream celebrities.

Bloggers - These popular writers build a community around their skill or expertise. They often write product reviews based on their personal experience. A Weibo post from an influential blogger will cost you between 100,000 and 300,000 RMB.

WeMedia (自媒体) - These are smaller media companies, often run by former or current journalists. They often appear to be a single individual yet there may be multiple people writing on a niche topic. The cost for a "WeMedia" Weibo post ranges widely from 1,500 to 60,000 RMB.

Industry-specific KOLs - This includes people like Wang Tao, a rally car driver and editor of AutoHome. These industry experts generally cost between 1,000 to 10,000 RMB per Weibo post.

Price and Payments

Weibo KOLs in general are cheaper than WeChat KOLs. Micro-KOLs on Weibo usually charge between 1,000 to 5,000 RMB (158 to 790 USD) per post. Mid-tier KOLs are likely to ask for a price ranging from 5,000 to 50,000 RMB (790 to 7,900 USD) per post. The most popular KOLs on Weibo charge much more; from 50,000 to 300,000 RMB (7,900 to 47,000 USD) per post and up.

Similar to KOLs on WeChat, Weibo KOLs usually take payment through Alipay and require 100% prepayment.

> *On Weibo, micro-KOLs typically have less than 100,000 followers, mid-tier KOLs average around 500,000 followers and top-tier KOLs have over 1 million followers.*
>
> —Kim Leitzes, Founder and CEO of PARKLU

Finding KOLs on Weibo

Apart from KOL search engines and KOL agencies, Weibo has a native search engine where users can find KOLs based on keywords, categories and locations.

In addition, Weibo also provides an official platform called "Wei Task" (微任务) to help users to find, select and engage KOLs in content promotion. On Wei Task, you can find and select registered Weibo bloggers to repost any commercial content. Before you find the KOLs you need to submit a simple plan indicating the price, content and posting time. If the blogger accepts the terms, he or she will promote the content based on your agreed schedule and get paid by the system once the task is completed.

"Wei Task" is a convenient gateway to KOL promotion. Since it's managed by Weibo, you can make sure all the content published is moderated to meet Weibo's regulations. However, due to automation, the platform does not advise you on which blogger is most suitable for your specific promotion. At times it may recommend ineffective or irrelevant bloggers.

Auditing a KOL

After you've identified matching KOLs, audit their profiles before entering into any cooperation.

A good KOL posts with a consistent tone and approach on a regular basis. You can check the comments and repost messages and the comments on previous promotion posts. They should be relevant to the original post. If the content is irrelevant, random or repetitive, there's a high possibility that the KOL has bought some fake interactions.

When you reach out to KOLs, ask them to give you a few examples of previous cooperations with other brands and the corresponding statistics. Be aware that no KOL commits to KPIs. If you have strict KPI expectations, please communicate and agree on this with the blogger before paying for a promotion.

Working with KOLs on Weibo

After selecting the right KOLs for your business, there are several ways to cooperate with them including:

Sponsored posts - These are like traditional paid media ads, except the content is created by the KOL and written in their voice. All you have to do is provide the KOL with a content outline and other material related to your product, services or campaign. It currently seems that any links to e-commerce sites other than Alibaba properties are difficult to post.

Product reviews - These are best if your KOL is an expert in a certain field.

Campaign launches - The most common type of campaigns for KOL cooperation are giveaway campaigns. They usually require users to follow the account, forward a designated post and/or mention several friends at the same time to win gifts.

Social selling - This is getting more popular among Chinese KOLs. New rules on Weibo require e-commerce links to Alibaba properties only and penalize posts that mention firms specializing in sales, marketing or advertising. Instead of receiving a fixed payment per post, KOLs are paid on a commission basis. That means the more clicks or sales they are able to help generate, the higher their commission.

Live streaming - These feature the KOL interacting with your brand or your product and can include links to enable viewers to purchase the item or get a discount.

In general, the KOLs will share a link to your website or product page when they are paid on a commission basis based on the number of clicks. It's a more direct way to increase revenue for brands compared to soft selling.

Tips

- The success of a Weibo KOL promotion can't be defined by any one variable or metric but it's common to use KPIs such as post views, reposts, comments, likes and follower growth to evaluate a KOL promotion.

- Use a mix of big and small KOLs.

- Do regular promotions with selected KOLs.

16.8 Weibo Advertising

Due to the increasing popularity of Weibo, advertisers are flocking to this platform for online brand advertising. Indeed, advertising on Weibo has always been the major revenue source for Sina. Their Q3 2017 financial results stated that advertising revenues increased 56% year over year to 364 million USD.

Compared to WeChat, Weibo offers more diverse and targeted advertising options for brands to increase exposure and reach out to focused market demographics. The four major advertising options are Display Ads, Weibo Search Engine Promotion, Fan Headlines and Fan Tunnel. It's important for brands to tailor a strategy for each type. A combined approach often works best.

1. **Display Ads**, also known as banner ads, are featured on the Weibo home page, on the search page of the "Discover" section, and on the side of users' newsfeeds.

    Advertisers can choose various ad sizes and placements across the web and mobile versions. You can select keywords to control their visibility based on user searches and have them displayed on relevant accounts. All these parameters determine the final cost.

    When users click the display ad, they will be directed to the advertiser's landing page so they're effective for driving traffic to an external link. They are usually for promoting events, sales or other campaigns.

 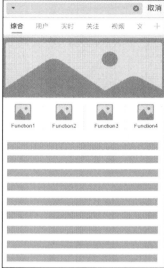

Display Ads   Search Engine
                            Promotions

2. **Fan Headlines,** also known as Fanstop (粉丝头条), are best for boosting your posts to existing followers to increase exposure and enhance engagement. Boosted posts appear once at the top of their newsfeed if they refresh the page in the next 24 hours. The boosted post features a "promoted" tag but otherwise, has the same format as regular posts. The price for each promotion depends on the number of current followers - the more followers you have, the more expensive it is.

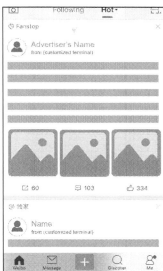

Fan Tunnel   Fan Headlines

3. **Fan Tunnel (粉丝通)** is a more targeted way for you to reach out to your target audience and collect followers. It offers more targeting options for you to promote your posts or your Weibo account. You can define the target audience by specifying age, gender, region, interests and even device types. At the same time, you can also target followers of other accounts with similar niches. Costs for Fan Tunnel promotions are typically calculated in CPM and pricing starts from 5 RMB per 1,000 exposures.

CHAPTER 17

How to Start Selling on Weibo

If you would like to sell your products on Weibo, one of the easiest ways is to insert a purchase link in your promotional post. This is this is the most widespread form of social media monetization in China.

Given that Alibaba owns a 31.5% stake in Weibo and it seems to have introduced a process to block links to sites that are not Alibaba properties, you'll need to set up an outlet on Tmall, Taobao, Alibaba or AliExpress before starting this phase.

Early in 2015, Weibo, in cooperation with two mainstream e-commerce platforms, Taobao and Jumei, launched shopping integration feature Weibo Window (微博橱窗). In 2016, the total number of Weibo Window users exceeded 1.3 million and its daily exposures reached 180 million.

17.1 Weibo Window

Weibo Window is an e-commerce function which allows users to set up a mini-store on their Weibo accounts. These shops are completely native to Weibo and they deep link to other Alibaba marketplaces.

Weibo Window is open to all users. In the user's Management Center, there is a tab labelled 'Weibo Window', where you can add products for sale. When you upload the product details, you need to input the purchase links to Taobao, Tmall and Jumei to finish this part of the process. You can further edit the information before publishing.

Once this is published, a new 'Weibo Window' section will be added to your page below your name card. Other users can check out your product list, read product reviews and make purchases.

17.2 Weibo Window Product Cards

Apart from adding products to Weibo Window, you can also create promotional posts with the product card feature. If you are using the desktop version, you just need to insert the URL of the product from Weibo Window and the post will showcase the product card automatically. If you are using the mobile application, you need to create the post by selecting the "Product" option. You can select any product in the Weibo Window section and create a post to promote it.

The promoted post appears similar to a regular one, but with a product card below it. The product card includes the product image, description and price. Users can click it for more details and to purchase it.

Meanwhile, you can also insert product cards into long articles. A long article that introduces your product with a featured product card can be great soft promotion. For each article, you can add up to 20 product cards.

Here are some recommendations when you create a post featuring product cards:

1.   Add personalized images or videos in your promotional post to attract attention.

2. Don't forget to attach the hashtag #WeiboWindow# (微博橱窗) or other hot hashtags to increase exposure and make your post more searchable on Weibo.

3. Launch giveaway campaigns to stimulate interactions and boost sharing.

4. Encourage your customers to share their purchases on Weibo to increase exposure and word-of-mouth.

CHAPTER 18

How to Do Your CRM with Weibo

18.1 Interacting with Followers

As Weibo is an open platform for sharing and discussion, it's important for brands to communicate and interact with followers proactively and in a personalized way. Good interactions can help to increase your follower loyalty, boost shares and conversions, create a positive image and lead to greater exposure. Below are some good practices for communicating and interacting with followers on Weibo.

Welcome Message

If your Weibo account is verified, it automatically sends out a welcome message to users once they follow the account. The default message is in Chinese and can be translated to "Thank you for following our account," but brands can pay 5,000 RMB to customize this auto-message. A customized welcome message should include a company introduction, detail what users can expect from the account and have a call to action. If you have a presence on other social media, don't forget to share those links in your welcome message to cross-promote.

Replying to Messages and Comments

In China, social media like Weibo plays an important role in customer service, as Chinese consumers often find it more convenient to communicate with brands via social media. If you receive any private messages, respond promptly to show that you care. If you don't have a dedicated person to monitor enquiries, set up an auto-reply to direct them to other communication channels.

To build a closer relationship with your followers, be friendly, personable and reply to as many comments as possible. If you receive a positive review or recommendation, make sure you show appreciation. When you receive negative comments or complaints, address the problem clearly and apologize when necessary. Be genuine and sincere when dealing with any issues. For bigger issues, assign your customer support team to contact the user to discuss the problem.

Reposting Fan Mentions

When users mention and tag your brand on Weibo, you will receive a system notification. Repost positive mentions on your page to promote relevant conversations and build your brand reputation.

Interacting with Related Weibo Accounts

There are lots of official accounts on Weibo, and you can easily find other accounts in the same industry or with similar niches. Follow related accounts to declare your presence and build relationships with them. You can also engage with other industry players on Weibo and comment on their posts. This helps to assert your expertise and get exposure to potential followers.

18.2 Managing a Crisis

You may receive complaints and negative comments on Weibo. No celebrity or brand is immune. When a crisis happens, address the issue quickly in a professional manner. Try not to dwell on these situations too much, remain positive and remember that bad media is often better than no media.

Tips for Weibo crisis management:

- If you have the resources, assign a full-time staff member or hire an agency to constantly monitor your Weibo account. The team can then respond to any crisis quickly.

- Don't delete any negative comments, unless you're sure that they're spam. Empathize with the customer, be clear on how you plan to resolve the issue and apologize for any inconvenience caused. This will help rebuild loyalty and trust.

- Release an official statement on Weibo after the crisis has occurred. Also publish the statement on the company's website and other social media so everyone is aware.

- After the crisis, thank users for their patience and support with another official statement. Tell users what you have learned from the crisis and what measures you have taken to prevent the same situation from happening again in the future. The ultimate goal is to make your customers feel confident in your brand.

18.3 Fake Accounts / Zombie Fans

Bots and fakes are flourishing on social media everywhere. Weibo is no exception.

Zombie Followers

Fake accounts, so-called zombie followers, are accounts that aren't managed by real users. However, they aren't completely 'dead' as they can still follow others and even comment and repost. Some brands and bloggers buy these zombie bot followers to boost their "fan" base and make their account seem more relevant.

Zombie followers can be generated using software or bought online. On Taobao, the Chinese version of eBay, you can find numerous providers selling zombie followers for as little as 1 USD for more than 1,000 followers. Fake followers have various levels. For the high quality ones, users can even define parameters such as geographic location and gender, in order to make them look more 'real'.

Fake Interactions

In addition, fake interactions, such as likes, reposts, and comments can also be bought. Some accounts buy them in order to fabricate interactions, so they look popular with a higher engagement rate. And more often, they are bought to meet marketing KPIs.

In China, the term for them is "Wangluo Shuijun" (网络水军), which can be translated as "Internet Water Army". They're ghostwriters paid to post comments. Their main purpose is media manipulation. For example, Chinese companies employ them to post on social media to influence public opinion.

Spotting a Fake Account or Interaction

There is no universal way to identify a fake account, but usually zombie followers share these similarities:

- Account name: Fake followers usually have names made up of random numbers and English letters.

- Profile picture: Many fake accounts use low-resolution images as their profile picture or leave their profile picture blank.

- Weibo posts: It's obvious that a follower is fake if you check the first few posts of the account and the content is random and meaningless.

To judge whether the interactions of a particular post are real or not, you can click the "Repost" or "Comment" button to see the content in detail. Usually fake comments have a similar sentence structure and most of them have no relation to the original post.

Threats

Buying zombie followers or fake interactions does not bring actual marketing value and is a waste of resources. On one hand, Weibo conducts cleanup campaigns on inactive accounts on a regular basis, in order to provide a clean online environment and offer a more accurate assessment of brands' Weibo popularity. Accounts that buy zombie followers have a sudden, significant drop in followers and, in the worst cases, these accounts are deactivated by Weibo.

Buying zombie followers and fake interactions can also ruin a brand's reputation and credibility. People can spot fake accounts and interactions and many of them are turned off by these tactics. If they find accounts doing these things, they aren't motivated to follow or engage with them.

Be aware that there are plenty of zombie followers lurking on Weibo. Paying for fake followers is against Weibo's regulations but when promoting with KOLs, understand that they may have purchased fake interactions, such as likes and comments.

CHAPTER 19

Your Next Steps on Weibo

Part III is about Weibo, its different features and how it's being used. Weibo is a good choice for marketing and advertising primarily because of its open and public nature. Different types of Weibo ads and its search engine both ensure higher exposure for brands than on WeChat. In this sense, Weibo is an ideal platform for them to establish a good brand image, grow initial followers and develop new relationships.

Meanwhile, Weibo is a place where netizens gather for the latest news and discussions about trending topics, celebrity gossip and personal interests. As a result, information on Weibo changes fast and can spread exponentially. The upside is that it provides opportunities for brands to do hot topic marketing and gain more exposure. The downside is that negative news also spreads quickly when a PR crisis hits. In this sense, Weibo can be a useful social listening tool as well.

In Part I, three categories of brands were discussed based on their China market entry mode. They were international brands already in China, brands doing cross-border e-commerce and overseas brands serving Chinese visitors. In this chapter, we'll see how these three types of brands should use Weibo and the most relevant tools or functions for each type of brand.

1. International Brands Already in China

This term refers to brands that have already set up a legal entity in China. They have online stores, brick-and-mortar stores or both in mainland China. They employ local staff and are well-adapted to the local e-commerce ecosystem. These brands are already known to some Chinese consumers.

An Official Account and Weibo Wall

These brands usually have an official Weibo account and an official WeChat account. They manage both accounts at the same time as part of a combined social media marketing strategy. This ensures consistency of content on both platforms and drives followers to different platforms to enlarge their influence.

Regular content posting is essential to keep the audience updated and engaged. On Weibo, posts are much shorter and the content is much simpler, but finding a suitable language style, publishing diversified content and maintaining a regular posting schedule are still important. In time, they build a Weibo Wall filled with informative, diversified multimedia content.

Meanwhile, with an official account, brands can launch different kinds of marketing campaigns. It's an effective way to earn exposure, grow followers and increase their interaction rate on the platform.

Weibo Customer Service

Weibo is not really designed for customer relationship management (CRM), but the mass messaging function and the custom menu bar in the private message dialog box still play an important role in customer service.

When users have pre-sales or after-sales questions, they can quickly find information using the keyword auto-reply function in the menu bar. It's also good for brands to get first-hand feedback from users on their products and improve their performance.

Weibo Window

Weibo cooperates with Taobao and Tmall to conduct sales on the platform through Weibo Window. Both individual sellers on Taobao and brands that have official stores on Tmall can import product links from the two platforms and sell directly on Weibo. They can also manage all the items and purchasing orders on Weibo without leaving the platform.

2. Brands Doing Cross-Border E-Commerce

These brands offer their products via international retailers or suppliers. Even without an official legal entity in China, they can have a Weibo account. It's common for them to engage KOLs for their initial promotions.

KOL Weibo Posts

To let consumers know about a new product, it's common to partner with Weibo KOLs to contribute to a comprehensive brand introduction. There can be product reviews, product recommendations, comprehensive Weibo articles or several posts for different products, with links to Alibaba group sales platforms where the brand has already set up their official flagship store.

KOLs and Weibo Window

Another type of KOL cooperation involves offering specific products for sale on the KOL's Taobao store. As some KOLs are individual sellers themselves, their Taobao store offer a number of overseas products for sale. With Weibo Window, they can import product links for direct sale.

Official Account and Weibo Wall

When these brands have accumulated some customers, they often open an official account and start posting regular content for further promotion. If they want to raise awareness, they need to do this.

3. Overseas Brands Serving Chinese Visitors

These brands are physically located outside of China. Their goal is not to sell their products to consumers living in China. Instead, their objective is to attract Chinese visitors to enjoy and pay for their services. They can be brands in the hospitality industry like restaurants and hotels, or schools that want to attract international students from China.

They're likely unknown to most Chinese consumers and their biggest challenge is standing out from the crowd and getting noticed by outbound visitors.

Official Account and User-Generated Content Campaigns

Having an official account is often necessary. With an official account, it's much easier to launch UGC (user-generated content) collection campaigns. Overseas brands can encourage their Chinese customers to write short reviews or upload beautiful pictures on Weibo while mentioning the brand's official account or adding specific hashtags.

Weibo Advertising

Weibo offers a variety of advertising options, including banner ads, search engine promotion, Fan Tunnel ads, landing page ads, etc. Due to Weibo's open and public nature, ads also appear in potential followers' feeds and usually promise wide exposure.

Weibo ads usually drive users to a specific landing page such as a campaign page, an e-commerce site or a Weibo account so it's best to launch a campaign at the same time. Offering discounts or coupons are great ways to attract more users.

Live Streaming

Weibo has partnered with Yizhibo so users can live stream themselves or watch other live streams directly on Weibo. Live streaming offers the chance to show users a vivid, entertaining demonstration of your products and get them interested.

Overseas brands can invite Chinese KOLs for a free visit. They can host live streams to introduce their brand and showcase their services and facilities. They can also do lucky draw campaigns with special offers from the brand as prizes.

PART IV

The Future: Get Ready for New Retail

CHAPTER 20

New Retail and the Future of Commerce in China

Retail sales are a lynchpin in China's economic growth strategy. In order to boost consumption and improve the overall economy, both the government and large tech giants are doing their duty. In 2016, Alibaba introduced its 'New Retail' strategy, which many believe will rewrite the future of retail in China and beyond. But it's not only Alibaba. Tencent, JD.com and others are also shaping the commercial experience in China. This is leading to rapid change as well as growing rivalry.

The core rivalry in China's digital space is between Alibaba and Tencent. Retail and payment systems are at the heart of their competition.

20.1 Alibaba Group

Founded in 1999 by Jack Ma, Alibaba is a global tech giant operating the largest online and mobile marketplaces in the world. Its ecosystem comprises e-commerce, digital media, local services, logistics, payments, digital marketing and cloud computing. Their mission is to make it easy to do business anywhere and their goal is to build the future infrastructure of commerce.

Alibaba first started as an e-commerce business connecting buyers and sellers, benefiting from China's growing Internet population and underdeveloped brick-and-mortar businesses. Now, Alibaba is the largest online retailer in the world. In the fiscal year 2017, Alibaba's gross merchandise volume (GMV) reached 547 million USD and its Singles' Day sales are bigger than Black Friday and Cyber Monday combined.

New Retail

At Alibaba's 2016 Computing Conference, Jack Ma focused his speech on five areas that are being transformed by technology that will have a profound impact on the future. The list included new manufacturing (新制造), new finance (新金融), new technology (新技术) and new energy (新能源) with new retail (新零售) at the center.

New retail is Alibaba's strategy to redefine commerce by enabling seamless engagement between the online and offline worlds. It's not about converting online users into offline customers or vice versa. It's about building a retail ecosystem that blends online and offline channels in a unified way that features the consumer at the center, often in new and unexpected ways. With new retail, Alibaba aims to use their data and technology capabilities to digitally transform offline retail in China, which accounts for 82% of total retail volume.

The concept of a uni-channel is central to this strategy. In the past, uni-channel referred to companies that offered products only through one outlet, usually a brick-and-mortar store, that had limited advertising options – radio, TV, newspaper, etc. More recently, multi-channel and omni-channel marketing have made use of both online and offline marketing opportunities. The goal was to be ever-present in major online and offline channels to increase the likelihood of customer interaction. Many brands give a customer diverse and inconsistent experiences across those channels while a few put the customer at the center of these interactions and create a uniform experience.

> *China is going to be the world's largest consumption market and that engine is going to drive the world economy. If you miss China, you miss the future.*"
>
> —Jack Ma, Founder of Alibaba Group

A uni-channel, as Alibaba envisions it, refers not to a single channel but to a unified channel that puts the customer at the center. It merges online and offline offerings and makes all of them accessible to the customer in a seamless manner. This includes online platforms, brick-and-mortar stores, supply chains, financing options and more. It also means a presence online that mixes traditional online retail, social media and advertising in integrated and surprising ways rather than as a cool gimmick. It blurs the line between online and offline and redefines the role of one's online presence.

For merchants, this helps them to digitize and transform every aspect of the retail value chain from merchandising to logistics without needing in-depth tech knowledge and expertise themselves. It empowers them to stay relevant in the digital economy and provides innovative brand-building and sales boosting opportunities.

For consumers, they receive personalized feeds that closely match their purchasing preferences. not only based on previous purchases, but also ads clicked, terms searched, links shared with friends, physical stores visited, merchandise browsed, TV shows watched and more. The new retail model also aims for in-store quality customer service in the virtual world. Customers can 'try on' their desired items in virtual dressing rooms and get product recommendations directly from brands or popular influencers.

Alibaba used the occasion of the 2017 Double 11 Shopping Festival - which itself has transformed retail by being 18 times bigger than Amazon Prime Day and 2.5 times bigger than Black Friday and Cyber Monday combined - to showcase their vision.

Over 1,000 brands converted more than 100,000 physical locations into smart stores, allowing merchants to leverage data insights to deliver a more tailored shopping experience. Meanwhile, 60 pop-up stores were opened in 52 malls in collaboration with more than 100 brands from home and abroad, which curated consumer experiences specific to the brands and products. International brands like Gap, Bose and Casio, took part.

Based on experiences in these stores, this is what the future of retail looks like.

1 Smart Stores 天猫智慧快闪店

New retail stores can curate consumer experiences specific to brands and products. The major features of these stores include:

- A connection to an online payment system is established to enter the store. In Alibaba's case, financial services of affiliated companies, such as Ant Financial's Alipay, must be scanned to enter their smart stores and their Hema supermarkets.

- Price tags are electronic and prices vary in real time based on certain factors.

- Facial recognition technology is used to track customers. Discounts are offered on items they smile at or that they have searched for online.

- Items can be purchased for later delivery. Home delivery details don't need to be given as the system already has the purchaser's home address on record. Delivery in major cities in China is already very fast taking from 15 minutes to 3 hours.

- Customers can receive location-based store recommendations and discount notifications through their Taobao or Tmall app on their mobile devices, driving traffic to offline stores.

- Customers can try on apparel and makeup items virtually using what Alibaba calls a "magic mirror". With the help of RFID (radio-frequency identification) and AR (augmented reality) technology, the items are shown how they will look on an accurately measured avatar of you. This can also be used to see what furniture looks like in one's home or to tour properties overseas.

- Customers can scan images to get product information or collect coupons.

- Consumers can scan a QR code to purchase items from vending machines and have them delivered home with a few clicks.

- There are also innovative technologies like the Cloud Shelf, which is a screen that replaces shelves in a store. It uses RFID technology to track and identify product tags, show the item's availability, color options and customer reviews on Tmall. The customer can purchase the item by scanning the product's QR code.

- A customer's purchasing behaviour data, facial recognition information, mobile gamification usage, coupons, discounts, memberships and customer service history is all stored and tracked.

As of February 2018, some of these features are already being added to non-commercial spaces such as smart nursing rooms that are connected online so that mothers can find them more easily. The rooms are equipped with screens that can be used to look for childcare items such as diapers that can be purchased while the mothers use the room.

The aim for all this data collection and these innovations is to personalize the shopping experience. Eventually, each person's experience, from the ads they see to the prices they pay, will be determined by data on an

> *We believe online and offline should work together with the data, with customer experience. "*
>
> —Jack Ma, Founder of Alibaba Group

individual level and no two people will experience the same journey. All aspects of the consumer experience will also be seamlessly linked and operate in concert for the ultimate convenience of the consumer.

2 Tmall Neighbourhood Convenience Stores / LST Corner Stores 零售通

Alibaba's LST (零售通 / "retail integrated") initiative is different from Amazon's physical store push in that it can be leveraged for use by millions of neighbourhood convenience stores and mom-and-pop shops to digitize their businesses rather than only be used in Alibaba owned stores.

For example, the LST system can help the owner of a brick-and-mortar retail store to measure the demographics and purchasing behaviours of surrounding customers and then predict and recommend the most in-demand products for sales in that store. Their tech can be used for merchandising, inventory management and logistics to enhance their business operations.

Last August, Weijun Grocery (维军超市), a community grocery store beside Zhejiang University in Hangzhou, joined Alibaba's LST system and was later chosen as the first trial target for its "Tmall Corner Store (天猫小店)" franchise. According to an interview with the store owner in August this year, the sales volume had increased 45% from the previous quarter, while customer traffic had grown by 26%.

3 Retail as Entertainment

Modern Chinese e-commerce consumers are predominantly young and mobile-savvy so shopping isn't just about passively adding items to their virtual shopping cart. It's already become a social activity, a means of consuming content and, ultimately, a form of entertainment. This embraces live streaming, AI, big data, personalization, gamification and user-generated content.

For example, while people are eating lunch with their friends, they can scan a code in the restaurant, which is also a retail outlet, to get a discount on some new clothes. The clothes have been chosen specifically for them based on their data. They can try them on virtually, compare items with their friends, purchase them and have them delivered so that they will arrive at their home before they do later that day. Then, pictures of themselves with their new items can be sent to the brand to enter a contest and later be used in an advertising campaign.

> *Alibaba is developing new retail models that are transforming many retail experiences from the grocery story, the car dealership, the local convenience store and even the shopping mall. We are working with our brand partners to incubate the technology, so it can be leveraged by the entire retail industry."*
>
> —Erica Matthews, Head of Corporate Relations,
> Alibaba Group

Major 'See Now, Buy Now' online fashion shows have already taken place in 2016 and 2017 with brands like MAC, Guerlain, Pandora, TAG Heuer and Rimowa taking part. During these shows, the audience can do more than just watch. They can purchase outfits using a purchase link shown on the left side of the screen on Taobao or Tmall, or shake their phones to go to the product page if they were watching the show on TV.

4 Gamification

In 2016, after seeing the popularity of location-based augmented reality game Pokémon Go, Alibaba launched a gaming campaign called Catch the Cat (捉猫猫). The cat people were trying to catch was Tmall's mascot. Last year, 65 well-known brands such as MAC, L'Occitane, P&G, Disneyworld, Pizza Hut and KFC participated in this gaming campaign that encourages consumers to go to retail stores.

Alibaba continued the campaign in 2017. Users could access the game interface on the Taobao or Tmall app on their mobile devices to catch 170 different types of cats that appeared randomly. Most of the cats were related to a designated brand. Once caught, users could get a game card with a special discount or coupons that they could use when they made purchases in the brand's Tmall store.

Users could redeem certain prizes in offline stores if they got a special set of game cards. For example, users could get a free roast chicken with a Double 11 gift card and a KFC game card. Tmall's cat mascot was also featured in thousands of stores across China, such as Starbucks, where users could catch these virtual cats.

5 A Blurring of the Line Between Consumer and Advertiser/Influencer/KOL

This is already taking place at a certain level in China as many brands reward consumers for posting their purchases and taking part in campaigns but it's going to happen in more sophisticated and embedded ways offline in the future.

For example, at one of the pop-up shops that were part of the 2017 Double 11 Festival, after you bought an item, a photo studio in the shop had staff to quickly put on professional makeup and take your picture with the item using sophisticated lighting. The resulting photo was stylish, ad quality and campaign ready.

The consumer now becomes a mini-influencer and an active partner in social selling.

20.2 Tencent

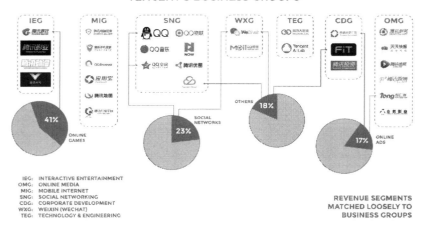

Infographic courtesy of China Channel

On November 8th, 2017, Tencent officially announced its 'Smart+' strategy with its cloud platform establishing a smart ecosystem covering retail, finance, logistics, marketing, communication and more in a decentralized way. Tencent also aims to execute Smart+Retail with the latest big data, cloud computing and AI technology. At the same time, existing WeChat functions such as official accounts, mini programs and WeChat Pay already support retail merchants. For instance, with the help of WeChat Pay and big data analysis, merchants can better understand their target consumers, and customize messages and promotions quite precisely. With mini programs, merchants can merge shopping experiences and output services of online and offline retail in a seamless manner.

On top of that, Tencent is cooperating with online retailers JD.com and Vipshop to power and finance its expansion, to build out its e-commerce and retailing capabilities and to enable it to better compete with Alibaba.

20.3 JD.com

JD started out as Jingdong Century Trading Co. Ltd, a traditional brick and mortar store in Beijing. Richard Liu started the company to sell CD ROM disks and drives. In 2003, during the SARS outbreak, when people were reluctant to leave their homes, Liu saw an opportunity, started selling his products online and JD.com was born.

It's now backed by Walmart and Tencent, who hold 10% and 20% stakes respectively, and is the second largest e-commerce platform in China. It controls 26.9% of the online B2C retail market, has 266.3 million annual active users and has 160,000 online merchants. It's net revenue in 2016 was 37 billion USD.

JD is also pursuing a similar strategy under the banner of 'Unbounded Retail' (无界零售). Similar to new retail, unbounded retail encompasses

4 concepts. Unbounded consumers can access more purchasing options through multiple providers and channels, even across space and time. Unbounded scenarios connect and combine online and offline channels and new scenarios. Unbounded supply chains cover the entire process from product design to delivery. Unbounded marketing has merchants and platforms collaborate to generate smart content and facilitate sales conversions.

JD's unbounded retail aims to use data and multiple channels to unify consumer experiences. For example, coupons released by JD can be used in the brand's online store on JD.com, on WeChat and in offline stores. Memberships and discounts can also be freely converted online or offline. It wants to create a seamless experience in various channels and help brands and consumers find each other more easily.

> *Tencent, mainly focusing on the businesses of social media, communication, digital content and financial services in the past, is willing to invest heavily in AI, cloud computing and big data.*"
>
> —Pony Ma, Founder of Tencent

Advances in AI will be used by JD.com to do things like generate unique homepages with a personalized selection of products and drive predictive logistics that chart consumer habits down to the level of individual communities and local neighborhoods. This would allow deliveries to be made within minutes of receiving an order.

JD.com opened its first commercial unmanned store in Shandong in January 2018 making it the first company in the world to launch an

unmanned store, beating Amazon and Alibaba. Shelves have cameras that can track and recognize products and in-store behavior. Facial recognition technology is used to track payments and products, allowing customers to skip checkout lines. What sets JD.com's unmanned stores apart from Alibaba's Tao Café and Amazon Go is that shoppers need not scan anything upon entry, allowing for a truly seamless experience.

20.4 Vipshop

Founded in 2008, Guangzhou-based Vipshop made a name for itself in flash sales and partnering with well-known, popular brands to sell extra inventory at a discount. It's now the fourth largest online marketplace after Tmall, JD and Suning with 3.8% of the market. It has 60.5 million active customers and its gross profit for Q3 2017 was 3.5 billion RMB (553 million USD).

Along with JD.com, Vipshop is a strategic ally of Tencent in their e-commerce battle with Alibaba. In December 2017, Tencent and JD.com announced their investment in Vipshop with Tencent taking a 7% stake and JD taking a 5.5% stake. The deal helps Tencent and JD access the site's young, female customer base and its valuable consumer data. Tencent will likely leverage WeChat and WeChat Pay as a part of this move.

20.5 Alibaba vs. Tencent

> *We plan to make use of artificial intelligence and robots to create a system that doesn't require human workers. This is going to cut our costs and improve our efficiency."*
>
> —Richard Liu, Founder of JD.com

Alibaba and Tencent are competing directly on multiple fronts now with social networking, e-commerce and payment systems at the centre of their battle.

Both companies have invested in areas as diverse as bike sharing services, online map providers, travel websites, brick and mortar retailers, cloud services and financial entities, with the names of their banking interests - WeBank and MYbank - being almost identical.

> *JD has been able to introduce many retail services that are unprecedented globally, including same and next day delivery as a standard for online orders nationwide, premium offline supermarkets, and seamless shopping via any channel that customers choose. Retailers in other markets are already looking toward our model because, up to now, this level of quality and speed has been seen as impossible to do profitably.*
>
> —Lori Chao, Director of International
> Communications, JD.com

In the case of WeChat versus Weibo, each network has managed to carve out its own territory after fierce competition and a phase that saw Weibo lose many users only to stage a comeback with a revised focus on entertainment and popular topics.

In terms of e-commerce, Tencent was lagging and Alibaba was clearly in the lead with its formidable Taobao and Tmall online marketplaces. Now, Tencent has partnered with JD and Vipshop and gained significant power in this area. JD seems to be particularly ambitious and is keen to innovate and expand.

In terms of payment services, both Tencent and Ant Financial, Alibaba's financial affiliate company, have significant support from authorities in China. They are trying to create a less cash dependent society and will also be using data from both payment systems in their upcoming social credit rating system, described in the next section.

Ant Financial's Alipay still has a larger share of online transactions than Tenpay, which includes WeChat Pay and QQ Wallet. However, Tencent has rapidly closed the gap in recent years leveraging the power of its dominant social network, WeChat. As of Q4, 2016, Alipay had a 55% share of online payments versus Tenpay's 37%.

And now they are not just competing at home. Both payment systems are accepted in South Africa, are being rolled out on a wide scale in Malaysia and have formed partnerships with local payment operators in Europe for use there. This is largely due to the huge monetary contribution of mainland Chinese tourists who are known for their desire to spend while on holiday.

To sum up, new retail and the commercial innovations from all the big players will definitely revolutionize and reshape the retail market and create novel and convenient experiences. The path will not be smooth however as many expect fiercer and fiercer competition to erupt between Alibaba and Tencent for control and domination of China's online space. This competition benefits consumers who will have more options, better prices and more convenience as these companies try to outdo each other.

TENCENT & ALIBABA: SOME KEY AREAS OF COMPETITION

AREA		TENCENT		ALIBABA
PAYMENTS		WECHAT PAY (PAY.WEIXIN.QQ.COM)	支付宝 ALIPAY	ALIPAY (ALIPAY.COM)
ECOMMERCE	JD.COM	JD, VIPSHOP (JD.COM, VIP.COM)	淘宝网 Taobao.com	TAOBAO, TMALL (TAOBAO.COM TMALL.COM)
SOCIAL		WECHAT, QQ (WEIXIN.QQ.COM, IM.QQ.COM)	新浪微博 weibo.com	WEIBO (WEIBO.COM)
BROWSERS	QQ Browser	QQ BROWSER (BROWSER.QQ.COM)	UC Browser	UC BROWSER (UCWEB.COM)
VIDEO	腾讯视频	TENCENT VIDEO (V.QQ.COM)	YOUKU 优酷	YOUKU, TUDOU (YOUKU.COM, TUDOU.COM)
RETAIL	永辉超市	YONGHUI, CARREFOUR (YONGHUI.COM.CN, CARREFOUR.CN)	苏宁	SUNING, HEMA (SUNING.COM, FRESHHEMA.COM)
CLOUD		TENCENT CLOUD (CLOUD.TENCENT.COM)	阿里云 aliyun.com	ALI CLOUD (ALIYUN.COM)
TRAVEL	LY.com	LY (LY.COM)	飞猪	FLIGGY (ALITRIP.COM)
BIKE SHARING	mobike	MOBIKE (MOBIKE.COM/CN)	ofo	OFO (OFO.SO)
ENTERPRISE PRODUCTIVITY		WECHAT ENTERPRISE, TIM (OFFICE.QQ.COM)	钉钉	DING TALK (DINGTALK.COM)
MAPS		TENCENT MAPS (MAP.QQ.COM)	高德地图 amap.com	AUTONAVI (DITU.AMAP.COM)
BANKING	WeBank	WEBANK (WEBANK.COM)	网商银行 MYbank	MY BANK (MYBANK.CN)
O2O ON-DEMAND	美团	MEITUAN DIANPING (MEITUAN.COM, DIANPING.COM)	口碑 饿了么	KOUBEI/ ELE.ME (KOUBEI.COM, ELE.ME)

Infographic courtesy of China Channel

However, for retailers and brands, things are more complex. These companies are each creating platforms and infrastructure that do not integrate with their competitors. So, although it's unclear which companies, platforms, apps and solutions will win out in the end, or what the ultimate effects of this intensifying rivalry will be, people will have to pick a side. There will be two camps with each hoping theirs comes out on top.

Social Ranking 2020

China is rolling out its Social Credit System which is highly integrated with technology, big data and the online world. Starting on July 1st, 2017, the government began generating an 18-digit Personal Identification Number for everyone in the country. This number is associated with what is, in essence, an economic and reputational identity card.

Credit scores were introduced about 70 years ago in the US and FICO scores are still used to determine a person's loan eligibility and interest rates in the United States.

China did not use similar credit systems or ratings until very recently and very few people in the country had access to them. So in the search for a system to fill this void, authorities have opted for a system that takes far more criteria into account. This new score, which takes into account a wide variety of online and offline behaviour, amounts to a credit score, background check, Google deep dive, Internet activity history, Yelp review, reference check and family interview all in one.

By 2020, all Chinese citizens will be enrolled in this vast national database. It will apply to Chinese individuals and businesses. At the moment, it's not clear whether foreign companies operating within China will be subject to the rating system or not.

The government's stated goal is to enhance trust and safety, particularly in regard to food, and to help enforce integrity in business. It hopes to influence higher rates of contract fulfillment and combat payment defaults, fraud and fake products.

Information will be stored on the country's unified credit information platform and will collect financial information (bank account, loan and mortgage data), business registration information, tax reports, social security payment statistics, traffic violation statistics, as well as records of commercial activity, social behavior, lawful and unlawful behaviour and online activity.

The programme was targeted for piloting in 12 cities: Hangzhou, Nanjing, Xiamen, Chengdu, Suzhou, Suqian, Huizhou, Wenzhou, Weihai, Weifang, Yiwu and Rongcheng. Local governments have announced that they have implemented the pilot scheme and stated that results have been positive.

The database has collected information from 44 government departments, all the provinces and cities, as well as over 60 private organizations. Two of the companies that were licensed to assist in the development of the system were Ant Financial's Sesame Credit (Zhima Credit), which rates users partly on their purchases through Alipay, and China Rapid Finance,

an online consumer lending platform and Tencent partner. Sesame Credit has also worked with taxi hailing service Didi Chuxing and Baihe, the country's largest online matchmaking service so it has had access to a very wide selection of data.

For those with high social credit scores, rewards may range from pre-approved loans of 5,000-50,000 RMB (788-7,880 USD) to depositless car rentals, faster hotel check-ins and fast-tracked applications for European Schengen visas. High scores have already become a status symbol in some circles and some have even boasted about their scores online.

Low scores may result in slower internet speeds, restricted access to restaurants, golf courses and private schools, the removal of the right to travel freely abroad or even restricted access to social-security benefits.

Certain jobs in the civil service, journalism and law may also be off limits. The principle has been adopted that if trust is broken in one place, restrictions will be imposed everywhere. People have raised concerns about this and want the system to take circumstances into account so that if, for example, someone misses a bill payment because they are ill in the hospital, it won't affect their score and punishments will not follow them.

The collaboration between the government and digital giants for social data provision initially raised concerns about consumer privacy. Some worry that monitoring their daily activities on social media, such as paying for a product or leaving a comment, will leave no personal space for a digital social life.

This rating system takes on new dimensions when considered along with the fact that China has the world's largest genome sequencing database. The China National GeneBank has over 500 million genetic sequences and the computational power and artificial intelligence to deal with them.

But many feel that establishing a more complete credit system will ultimately benefit Chinese citizens in terms of financial security. Utilizing the advantages of China's successful technology companies, big data, cloud computing and AI, China will be able to improve its social mechanisms, reinforce reputable behaviour and better integrate with developing global trends. There's also optimism for some in seeing China become, according to many, the world's most advanced tech nation.

CHAPTER 21

Technology and Shifting Epicenters

China has taken quite a journey to get where it is today. When the economic reforms of the late 1970s and early 1980s began, people saw China as a developing nation trying hard to catch up. Then, manufacturing centres began to pop up in Southern China and people saw it as a toy and knick knack factory. After that it was seen as the copying and pirating capital of the world.

Many didn't believe that a Communist country could transition to a wider market economy integrated with the rest of the world or move up the manufacturing chain to more complex products, but it did.

Although changes are taking place, such as rising wages and other countries expanding their manufacturing sectors, China won't lose its place as the world's factory any time soon. With the rise in manufacturing came a wealth of technology transfer and a great deal of tech-related industry. Now it's accomplishing what many thought was impossible. It's moving swiftly into the age of innovation and ahead of the rest of the world in some areas.

Shenzhen

Most of the world's computers and smartphones are made in factories in China and most of those factories are concentrated in and around the Pearl River Delta. The components for computers and other devices are largely made in China and, with rare exception, assembled there too. China is also the source of the bulk of the world's rare earth metals, a necessary component for smartphones and other digital devices.

At the centre of that is Shenzhen. A combination of manufacturing infrastructure, key resources, supply chains, powerful tech companies, startups, incubators and international transport and financial hub Hong Kong next door put it in a sweet spot. The region has been called a technopolis, Silicon Delta and the Chinese government now refers to it as the Greater Bay Area. It's emerging from a phase that saw ideas, visions and designs developed abroad with product and hardware execution done locally. Now, both are happening in the same place at record speeds and it's attracting local and international talent. Established brands are also making their mark globally.

For example, Lenovo is in second place for global PC sales behind legacy tech company Hewlett Packard. Shenzhen-based Huawei's global smartphone sales surpassed Apple's in 2017, putting it in second place behind Samsung, another Asian giant.

And it's not just manufacturing and sales. Homegrown tech companies are now on the global stage in terms of service, partnerships and brand recognition. Alibaba is a case in point. It entered the ring as a long-term Olympic sponsor in 2018, just as McDonalds exited. It provided cloud services, e-commerce platforms and digital media for the winter Olympics in Pyeongchang and is helping the IOC find ways to save money on future games. It also launched its first global ad campaign focusing on underdogs, sportsmanship and generosity. The company may have an interesting inside perspective in that the president of Alibaba Group,

For markets like the U.S., Europe, Japan, S. Korea and Australia, we are focused on helping brands, retailers and small businesses access the China consumer market. As incomes rise, Chinese consumers are looking for high-quality, imported products."

—Erica Matthews, Head of Corporate Relations,
Alibaba Group

Michael Evans, won an Olympic gold medal in rowing for his native Canada in 1984.

These developments are no accident. Local and national authorities are supportive and involved. The Guangdong provincial government's Guangzhou-Shenzhen Technology Innovation Corridor Scheme aims to further integrate and promote infrastructure, supply chains, technology and innovation. And it's not only Shenzhen and Guangdong that are involved. Beijing, Shanghai and Hangzhou are also in the game in the same way that US cities outside of San Francisco, such as New York (Silicon Alley), Portland (Silicon Forest) and Austin (Silicon Hills) are. According to some, Beijing is the top tech hub in the world followed by Berlin with San Francisco in third place. The central government is also supporting cities like Guiyang and Chengdu as they build tech hubs.

While still behind in some areas, 2018 was a coming out party for some big national brands and it's clear that the age of innovation has arrived in China. The evolution is obvious and unstoppable.

So what does this look like in terms of facts and figures and real world examples as of 2018?

Supercomputing

- In 2017, China had the fastest supercomputers in the world for the 8th year in a row. 2016 was the first time their computers used only Chinese designed processors. China had 202 of the world's 500 fastest supercomputers - including the top two - compared with the US's 143. The top American computer ranked 5th behind China, Switzerland and Japan. This was China's biggest lead in 25 years. China intends to launch a new generation of exascale supercomputers in 2018. These machines are sometimes described as super supercomputers and are capable of a billion billion calculations per second.

The Blockchain

- Blockchain technology puts blocks of signed, time-stamped data in a chain to create a record of transactions and processes. It's encrypted with passwords, distributed across a network and unchangeable. It's like a set of digital fingerprints. This has made the technology ideal for things like digital contracts, secure tracking procedures, peer to peer transactions and online banking. This is why many companies and governments are investing in and researching the technology with a view to applications that can increase security, speed and services offered digitally.

- Blockchain technology saw its first official mention in China in 2016, when it was written into the Communist Party's 13th Five-Year Plan. The government wants China to be a frontrunner in the technology's development and wants to apply blockchain technology to industry and commerce. It's also widely accepted that in China, this will be done in a highly controlled way that maintains the current ban on ICOs, bitcoin and other cryptocurrencies while focusing on increasing the technology's security for potential later use in finance.

- According to one report, 550 blockchain technology-related patents were filed by companies in China as of 2017, versus 284 from the US and 192 for South Korea.

- It's been noted that various city and provincial governments are already getting on the development bandwagon by proposing guidelines to attract firms that design, develop and implement blockchain applications. Hangzhou, Chengdu, and Guangxi have already expressed interest and proposed policies to encourage research and development in the field.

AI

- Chinese startup Cambricon has designed a novel chip architecture that can enable portable consumer devices to engage in the same level of AI that took 16,000 microprocessors to accomplish in 2012. This would make them capable of recognizing faces, navigating roads and translating languages. In the worldwide search for AI-enabled chips, the Chen brothers who founded Cambricon are leading the way and their chip has already been used in a Huawei smartphone that they called the world's first "real AI phone". Cambricon was valued at 1 billion USD at the time of writing.

- China is investing heavily in AI, from chips to algorithms and the State Council has issued an ambitious policy for the nation to become "the world's primary AI innovation center" by 2030.

Robotics

- China is the fastest growing and largest robotics market in the world. It is currently ranks No. 1 in sales for industrial robots. South Korea and Japan are ranked second and third, respectively and the U.S. is fourth. The global robotics market is worth about 30 billion USD and by 2019, China will account for 40% of total worldwide robotic sales, an increase from 27% in 2015.

- In 2015, China's government devised the Robotics Industry Development Plan as part of an industry initiative called Made in China 2025. This five-year plan aims to rapidly expand the robotics sector. China wants to be able to manufacture at least 100,000 industrial robots per year by 2020. This is being done with research and development as well as acquisition and investment. For example, Chinese home appliance maker Midea Group acquired a majority stake in the German robot manufacturer Kuka GA last year and Israeli motion solutions provider Servotronix Motion Control so that it can integrate their technologies into its robotics.

Drone Technology

- The world leader in civilian drones is Shenzhen-based DJI (Dajiang Innovations Ltd.) which has captured 70% of the market. Their unmanned aerial vehicles (UAVs) are optimized for photography and filming. They have a large, avid fan base. Their aerial photography technology has been used on productions like American Ninja Warrior, The Amazing Race and Game of Thrones and the company has won an Emmy for its engineering creativity.

- Several of the major players in Chinese e-commerce, such as Alibaba, Tencent and JD.com, have drone delivery programs at advanced stages of development and the first official government license for drone deliveries was granted to SF Express, China's largest logistics firm, in March 2018. This will impact remote areas of the country as well as allowing a rapid response in cases of emergencies or natural disasters.

Financial Technology

- In 2017, Chinese fintech (financial technology) firms took the top three spots and five of the top ten spots in KPMG and H2 Ventures' Fintech 100 list. The list ranks firms from around the globe based on innovation, capital-raising activity, size and reach. This was the second year in a row for Alibaba affiliate Ant Financial to top the list.

The Internet of Things

- The bike-sharing services in major cities in China are examples of how 'the internet of things' is spreading through the country. The bikes, belonging to a variety of startups and widely used, are unlocked, tracked and paid for via apps and using GPS technology. This initiative is also part of the push in China to improve air quality by making bikes easy alternatives to more polluting forms of transport. This area is also pushing forward the use of 5G technology and battery life improvements.

Virtual Reality (VR)

- Virtual reality tech has been embraced in China. In 2016, sales of VR headsets accounted for 59.2% of the total for virtual reality-related revenue in China while consumer content made up just 7.7%. However, consumer VR content is set to explode, and is expected to account for 35.3% of all VR revenue by 2021 with games leading the VR content category, generating 9.62 billion RMB (1.45 billion USD) followed by films and movies at 8.79 billion RMB (1.32 billion USD).

- CCTV, China's state-owned broadcaster, has adopted VR technology from a Beijing-based production startup to telecast the Spring Festival Gala and basketball matches. The startup, 7D Vision Tech, has made about half of its 20 million RMB in annual sales (2.9 million USD) in service fees for VR filming for TV stations.

Medical Big Data

- China is the global center for medical studies and data. This is due to its large population and its desire to improve its medical technology and its healthcare system as a whole. It's about the only place in the world that researchers can quickly pool information on 100,000 patients. Several key startups specializing in health tech are engaged in partnerships in China to find new interventions for illnesses and to perfect algorithms for use in medical artificial intelligence.

- As mentioned earlier, China also has the world's largest genome database, making it a centre for genomic research and data. Some medical research and experiments using cutting edge technology have also occured there that generated heated debate. In 2015, Chinese researchers successfully edited genes for the first time in an experiment that saw them remove two puppy embryos from their mother, edit their genes to make them build muscle faster, then reinsert them into their mother. In 2017, it also successfully cloned dogs that had had their genes edited previously.

Green Energy Technology

- Solar panel manufacturing is dominated by China, which has been the world's largest manufacturer since 2008. China is also the world leader in wind power generation. It has the largest wind power capacity of any nation and is still growing. China's 13th Five Year Plan for Building Energy Efficiency and Green Building Development includes aggressive goals for green building construction and renovation, including a requirement for 50% of all new urban buildings to be certified green buildings.

Electric Vehicles

- China is the largest car market in the world and the largest car producer. It's also the largest market in the world for electric vehicles and is in the lead in terms of electric vehicle production and investment. Local manufacturers do not sell the majority of traditional vehicles within the country yet but domestic companies have a 90% market share in the electric vehicle arena.

- The Chinese government offers rebates of up to 15,000 USD to buyers of electric vehicles, has threatened to block automakers that don't make electric vehicles and is setting up charging stations across the country.

- "It's clearly the case that China will lead the world in EV development," William C. Ford Jr., the executive chairman of Ford Motor Company.

- "Sometimes people are under the impression that China is either dragging their feet or somehow behind the U.S. in terms of sustainable energy promotion, but they are by far the most aggressive on earth." Elon Musk.

Space Exploration

- In 2013, China joined the US and Russia to became one of only 3 nations that can send both satellites and people into space and is capable of a soft moon landing. The China National Space Administration has sent numerous satellites into space and has partnered with Russian and European space agencies in various projects, including preparations for a manned mission to Mars.

- The China National Space Administration has set its sights on a moon landing by 2025, and is developing plans and capabilities for supersonic aircraft as well as high powered lasers that will test the bounds of physics and engineering theory and practice.

What do these advancements mean for the world of commerce and e-commerce? Here are some examples.

JD.com

JD uses VR and AR e-commerce apps and has formed an alliance between the e-commerce industry and over 30 VR and AR companies that will innovate in this area to develop common tools and standards. These apps allow shoppers to experience products in the virtual world or interact with the brand in a way that mixes online and offline worlds. For example, virtual reality technology can be used to view a piece of virtual furniture in a shopper's living room at home. They've also set up a live streaming shopping channel that incorporates virtual reality. Shoppers can use VR goggles to interact with products in a 3D environment, purchase the item and arrange for delivery all within the app.

They are committed to developing in this area and are also creating solutions behind the scenes in their manufacturing and supply chains. If a worker is doing detailed work, they could use a VR app to magnify the item they are working on.

They also announced on March 2nd, 2018 that they will use blockchain tech to track Australian beef from source to delivery in China in cooperation with Australian exporter InterAgri. This technology is a step up from RFID tracking technology. Unlike RFID chips, the blockchain records are more reliable and efficient and don't require hardware, such as chips, to be embedded in products. This also allows consumers to access detailed information about the source of their products.

JD is also a pioneer in terms of fast and innovative delivery and has made drone delivery a reality in China. JD.com has drones that can carry 1 ton of cargo up to 300 km and has been granted permission by the Shanxi provincial government to operate hundreds of low altitude drone routes covering almost 30,000 sq km. This provides service to remote regions and enables rural residents to more easily sell their products in cities. The company plans to increase it services for rural areas and maintain its position as a world leader in advanced delivery systems.

Alibaba and Tmall

Like JD.com, they want to give customers a greater ability to examine products and test them out in real and virtual environments through VR/AR. They also live stream VR entertainment with an e-commerce focus

> *We are the platform, not the retailer. So when brands want to link their consumer data, inventory and logistics between their online store and physical stores, it's possible for two main reasons. First, the largest e-commerce platform is their partner, not a competitor. And second, they don't have to convince consumers to download their app."*
>
> —Erica Matthews, Head of Corporate Relations,
> Alibaba Group

in connection with special events like the company's annual Singles' Day sale. It's also investing in virtual reality and augmented reality in the entertainment realm and has ventures like the newly established GnomeMagic Lab to create VR content for its movie and TV units.

In terms of blockchain technology, Alibaba has partnered with logistics company Cainiao to track cross-border goods using blockchain processes. This includes information on the manufacturer, port of dispatch, delivery and arrival. This is in keeping with modern supply chain innovations and helps to ensure product safety, which is paramount to Chinese consumers.

They are also using drones to deliver items to remote or hard to reach locations. In October, 2017, Alibaba used drones to deliver packages over open water for the first time. The flying robots delivered six boxes of fruit from Putian, Fujian to nearby Meizhou Island – a distance of 5.5 kilometres. Alibaba said it would consider using the drones in the future to deliver high value products such as medical supplies and fresh food. Delivery systems like this mean that in the future, there may be few locations in the country that are unreachable.

Alibaba is also bringing legacy industries and manufacturers to the e-commerce world. In late 2017, Alibaba started a partnership with Ford to sell their vehicles online on Tmall. The partnership provides their cars for extended test drive experiences and for purchase via car vending machines. Their first car vending machine opened in March, 2018 in Guangzhou. Users pay a deposit, schedule a test drive online and use photos and facial recognition tech to prove their identity when picking up their car. If they decide to buy, they can visit a car dealership afterward to pay for the vehicle.

Ford is very interested in using big data from the venture to monitor sales trends and using Tmall's massive database of information on consumers. In 2016, 1 million vehicles, worth a whopping 15 billion USD, were sold online in China. On Singles' Day, the annual shopping bonanza created by Alibaba, 100,000 cars were sold on its Taobao and Tmall shopping platforms.

These are just a few of the examples of how advancing technology and new approaches are changing e-commerce but there will be many more in the coming years.

China Going Global

As mentioned before, China's path to where it is today has had many phases. It's gone from a place shut off from the world, to a manufacturing centre, to a place that Western companies coveted for its huge consumer base. Then China developed its own companies that were outside the state-owned system. These companies succeeded within China and now, contrary to the predictions of many, are succeeding and becoming known globally. Additionally, Chinese business interests are acquiring foreign companies and taking on global assets.

Chinese Brands Known Globally

Aside from brands that have already been discussed in detail, such as Alibaba, WeChat and others, here are some examples of local Chinese brands, largely unknown outside of the country ten years ago, that are now players on the global stage.

Lenovo

Lenovo is the second largest PC manufacturer in the world, the largest seller of smartphones in China and a known brand name globally. Once a small company known only for its cheap computers, it acquired and merged with other technology companies and is now a conglomerate with headquarters in Beijing and Morrisville, North Carolina. It started to become an international name when it acquired IBM's personal computer division in 2005 and owns the Thinkpad brand. It now also owns two lines of servers first made by IBM, Motorola Mobility as well as German and Brazilian tech interests. Most of its acquisitions were made to help it gain access to international markets.

Huawei

Huawei is a multinational telecommunications company with headquarters in Shenzhen, China. It is the largest telecommunications manufacturer in the world. It supplies equipment for and builds telecommunications infrastructure globally. This includes traditional phone technology as well as internet service equipment and technology and cloud services. Most of the world's largest providers have worked with Huawei at some point including British Telecom, Vodafone, T-Mobile, Portugal Telecom and Bell Canada. It also has a successful smartphone division that plans to launch one of the world's first 5G handsets and may have plans to launch a blockchain enabled phone. It is a world leader in 5G technology and designs its own chips.

Haier

Haier is a multinational consumer electronics and appliance company with headquarters in Qingdao, Shandong. It was a pioneer in China's globalization drive and was one of the first Chinese companies to successfully expand into international markets. It has been the largest home appliance company in the world for 8 years in a row in terms of market share with 10.3% of the market in 2016 according to Euromonitor International. It is known for having business strategies that are unlike other large corporations and constantly updating its approaches. It recently bought GE Appliances and is focussing on its e-commerce presence and internet connected products.

Hisense

Hisense is similar to Haier in that it's also a large white goods and electronics manufacturer based in Qingdao. However, it may be one of the lesser known names on this list in terms of its major product lines as it sells under a variety of brand names that it has acquired through company acquisitions, partnerships or brand licensing deals. It has purchased product lines and selling rights to products from Sharp, Hitachi, NEC, Sanyo, Toshiba and Qualcomm. The Hisense name may be better known for its smart TVs, smartphones as well as its high profile sports-related promotional endeavors such as the naming rights to the Hisense Arena in Melbourne, sponsorship of the Euro 2016 football championships and its FIFA partnership. It's a state-owned company that has some publicly traded subsidiaries.

Xiaomi

Xiaomi made its name as a mobile phone manufacturer and was a key player as smartphones were becoming more popular. It suffered some setbacks in recent years but has staged a comeback and is a globally known name in the smartphone sector. It's the fifth best-selling smartphone in

China (just behind Apple), the second largest seller in India and ranks in the top 10 worldwide.

Anker

Anker, founded in 2011, based in Changsha with offices in Shenzhen and Seattle, is one of the world's most popular brands for portable power banks. It was one of the first brands to master this product category by selling on Amazon. Outside of China, it still channels its sales and delivery operations there. Within China, it sells on Tmall and JD.com. Its products regularly feature in top 10 lists of the best rechargers. It is now branching out into new product areas such as portable projectors and equipment for smart homes.

DJI

DJI was founded in 2006. Its founder, Zhejiang's Frank Wang, was a student at the Hong Kong University of Science and Technology which gave him a grant to study and develop drone technology. With headquarters in Shenzhen, it's world renowned for its unmanned flying machines that are optimized for photo and filming purposes. Its products have a large amateur following in addition to good standing in the world of TV and film, where the company has won a technology Emmy. It has 66 percent of the North American market share for drones between 1,000-2,000 USD and 67 percent in the 2,000-4,000 USD range.

OnePlus

The youngest brand on this list, it was founded in 2013. Although it portrayed itself as a rebellious startup, one of its founders is the former vice president of Oppo, a major brand in Chinese smartphones, and Oppo is its primary, and only institutional, investor. (Its first phone was called the OnePlus One which is abbreviated as OPO.) The brand made its mark by initially selling only via pre-sale and only on the internet. This led to the development of a dedicated online following. Its phones were flagship quality but at a much lower price. It still operates that way today with the exception of invitations and pre-sales. Its phones have evolved and are still competitive with the most advanced phones on the market.

Global Brands Now Owned by Chinese Companies

These brands were founded and came to prominence in markets outside of China and are strongly connected with certain countries, nationalities, philosophies or lifestyles. It might come as a surprise to some readers that they are now owned by Chinese companies.

- IBM Thinkpad - Owned by Lenovo.
- Motorola Mobility - Owned by Lenovo
- General Electric Appliances - Owned by Haier
- Volvo cars - Owned by Zhejiang Geely Holding Group
- London Black Cabs - Owned by Zhejiang Geely Holding Group
- Club Med - Owned by Fosun International Ltd.
- Inter Milan - Majority owned by Suning Holdings Group
- AC Milan - Majority owned by Chinese company Rossoneri Sport Investment Co.
- Aston Villa - Majority owned by Chinese company Recon Sports Limited
- The Waldorf Astoria - Owned by Anbang Insurance Group
- The Ironman Triathlon - Organizer Worldwide Triathlon Corporation is owned by Wanda Group
- Pizza Express - Owned by Chinese private equity firm Hony Capital
- Harvey Nichols - Owned by Dickson Concepts
- Grindr - Owned by game developer Beijing Kunlun Tech

- Corbis Image Licensing - Founded by Bill Gates, now owned by Unity Glory International, subsidiary of the Visual China Group, the exclusive distributor for Getty Images in China

- 500px - popular photo site similar to Flickr, now owned by Visual China Group
- AMC Theatres - Owned by Chinese conglomerate Wanda Group. This acquisition made Wanda Group the owner of the largest theatre chain in the world
- Legendary Entertainment, producer of films like Batman Begins, The Dark Knight, Inception, Godzilla, Steve Jobs and Straight Outta Compton, - Owned by Wanda Group

Soft Power

Part of this move into globalization has been an increasing focus on and facility with soft power and projecting China's image worldwide through narratives that are very different from the past. Part of this is having Chinese brands, personalities, expertise and technology becoming commonplace outside of the country and part of this is having a say in areas such as international movie production and the world of Hollywood.

Some of this soft power is being achieved through business partnerships. There is more and more cooperation with Western companies who are not just seeking access to the huge Chinese market, as in the past, but also seeking access to Chinese technology, business methods, deep pockets or expertise in new product areas.

In one example, Mobike, the world's largest smart bike sharing service, is partnering with AT&T to support its proprietary smart locks with built-in GPS and Internet of Things (IoT) technology as it rolls out in some US markets. Mobike's technology, aims and business model fit in well with urban areas that want to develop their smart city capabilities, push green initiatives or promote exercise.

In another example, Walmart and JD.com first announced a strategic alliance in June 2016 and launched the first JD-Walmart 8.8 Shopping Festival in 2017. The day's combined transaction volume for Walmart on JD.com increased 13 fold and Walmart's physical stores also saw significant traffic growth.

As Walmart and Tencent hold stakes in JD.com, the three have also worked together in other areas. For example, Walmart and JD.com coordinated their membership programs to accept WeChat Pay payments, offer discounts and benefits across both retailers and have developed a system to allow JD.com to fulfil orders with Walmart's inventory.

Chinese celebrities in entertainment, sports and even the business world are more and more widely recognized around the world and China's involvement with Hollywood and the global entertainment world is increasing. Some traditional sources for film funding have changed and filmmakers and producers are looking for investors in new markets. At the same time, Chinese companies are looking to extend their reach and make key investments and acquisitions.

For example, STX Entertainment is an independent American film and television studio that is backed by Tencent Holdings and PCCW. The studio also works with Alibaba Pictures, the entertainment arm of Alibaba Group. At the Academy Awards in March, 2018, Canadian actor Christopher Plummer was nominated for a best actor Oscar in the STX backed film All the Money in the World.

2017 saw a great deal of film co-productions along with media investments and acquisitions involving major Chinese companies. It also saw plenty of films aimed at Chinese audiences that were hoping to get a slice of China's box office. Although China's box office takings aren't higher than North America's yet, many think they will be soon. Films also still depend on foreign box office numbers to make a profit. The most famous, or infamous, example of this trend had to be the movie The Great Wall, starring Hollywood actor Matt Damon in the lead.

Although the Chinese government has recently clamped down on foreign investment in the entertainment field, the trend continues from the West with some directors, such as Renny Harlin (Die Hard 2, Cliffhanger) departing Hollywood in favour of China.

In another change from the past, when stars had lucrative, secret promotional partnerships in Asia, famous names are no longer shy about declaring their Asian and Chinese presence and activities. Nicole Kidman, Pharrell Williams, Jessie J and the Blue Man Group all attended Alibaba's Singles' Day Gala in 2017. Pharrell Williams even co-wrote a song just for the event which he sang with Chinese Canadian singer and actor Kris Wu. In another notable example, Victoria's Secret's annual fashion show was in Shanghai in 2017.

It's even been said that the Spice Girls are finally reuniting. Not for a tour and not for a TV show in their homeland, but as part of an extensive deal that features them being judges on a Chinese reality TV talent show.

Another big example from 2018 was Alibaba's involvement in the winter Olympics and its global advertising campaign on the back of that. This is a long term commitment and it seems that Alibaba has no intentions of going anywhere. At Alibaba's Gateway 17 conference in Detroit in 2017, Jack Ma predicted that by 2035, his company will generate enough income to make it the world's 5th largest economy.

These changes, challenges, transitions and catalysts are affecting China and the whole world. I strongly encourage all of you to stay in the loop. Be curious and open-minded. Learn and adapt to the latest technology and social trends. These are the skills we will all need for the coming decades to stay relevant in any field, especially when working with China.

Acknowledgements

This book has been a team effort, and I'm grateful to the many people who have helped me make it reality. First and foremost a big thank you goes to the wonderful Alarice team that contributed writing, research and their many talents: Mason Ku, Jackie Chen, Sammi Wong and Susie Hu.

To my fantastic editor, Maureen Lea, who made this book readable :)

To my husband, Marius, for always being there for me, no matter what I was doing.

With special thanks to:

Erica Matthews from Alibaba Group
Lori Chao from JD.com
Matthew Brennan from China Channel
Kim Leitzes from ParkLU
Mirko Wormuth from OmniChannel China
Joseph Leveque from 31Ten
Thomas Meyer from Mobile Now Group
Thomas Graziani from WalktheChat
Sheng Pang from Juplus
Andrew Schorr from Grata
Miranda Tan from Robin8

Appendix

1. China's Social Media Landscape

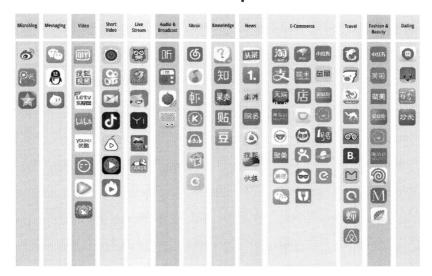

2. Marketing Strategies for WeChat and Weibo

	WeChat	Weibo
Increase exposure	Interactive H5 KOL promotion UGC + incentives Unique content	Intensive ads KOL promotion Creative video Live streaming
Increase sales	WeChat ads KOL crossover Exclusive coupons + discounts	Campaigns + Weibo Window KOL promotion codes KOL trial Live streaming with "Watch and Buy"
Increase followers	Lucky draws UGC + incentives KOL promotion	Lucky draw UGC + incentives KOL live streaming

3. List of KOL Agencies

Name	Website	Service	Platforms
Antipodal Talent	www.antipodal.com	KOL and Internet Celebrity Talent Management, KOL Marketing Strategy, KOL Live Streaming Campaign Management.	Weibo, WeChat, Yizhibo, Youku, Huajiao, Inke, Miaopai, Taobao, Tencent TV, etc.
AisaKOL	www.asiakol.com	KOL Research, KOL Management, KOL Marketing Campaigns, KOL Marketing Strategy, KOL Database, etc.	Weibo, WeChat, Meipai, Yizhibo and other live streaming platforms.
Gushan Culture (鼓山文化)	http://www.weibo.com/3877848191	KOL Management	WeChat and Weibo.
iconKOL	www.iconkol.com	KOL Search, Customized KOL Marketing Campaign, KOL Database, etc.	
KOLSTORE	www.kolstore.com	KOL Search, KOL Database, etc.	WeChat and Weibo.
Louis Communication (楼氏传播)	www.loushijt.com	KOL Management	Weibo, WeChat, Meipai.
媒界PRAD	www.myprad.com	KOL Search, KOL Contact, KOL Database, Internet Celebrities recommendations, etc.	WeChat, Inke, Huajiao and Yizhibo.
ParkLU	www.parklu.com	Self-service and full-service options with a ParkLU subscription include KOL Research, KOL Campaign Management, KOL Content Strategy, KOL Database, Brand Ambassador Recruitment and Management, Top-tier and Mid-tier KOL Engagement, KOL network coverage for Mainland China, Hong Kong and overseas Chinese KOLs.	WeChat, Weibo, Youku, Meipai, Yizhibo, Inke, Xiaohongshu, Meilimeizhuang, Nice, Instagram.

Robin 8	www.robin8.net	KOL Search, KOL Database, etc.	Weibo, WeChat, Zhihu, Miaopai, Meipai.
Socially Powerful	www.sociallypower-fulmedia.com	KOL Research, KOL Management, KOL Marketing Campaign, KOL Marketing Strategy, KOL Database, etc.	Weibo, WeChat, RenRen, QZone, YouKu, Tudou, etc.
Toutiao KOL	www.toutiaokol.com	KOL Search, KOL Database, etc.	Toutiao
Yaxian Advertising (牙仙广告)	http://www.weibo.com/5331861515	KOL Management	WeChat and Weibo.

4. Classification of Cities in China by Development Level

Special Administrative Regions - Hong Kong and Macau

Tier System*

First Tier	Beijing, Shanghai, Tianjin, Guangzhou, Shenzhen
Second Tier	Nanjing, Hangzhou, Suzhou, Wuhan, Xi'an, Shenyang, Chengdu, Chongqing, Xiamen
Third Tier	Jinan, Hefei, Dalian, Harbin, Changsha, Zhengzhou, Shijiazhuang, Fuzhou, Taiyuan, Urumqi, Qingdao
Fourth Tier	Kunming, Guiyang, Nanchang, Lanzhou, Yinchuan, Nanning, Xining, Changchun, Hohhot, Baoding, Ningbo, Datong, Weihai, Shantou, Lhasa and Haikou, all provincial capitals etc.

* These designations change from time to time based on rapid economic change and the weighting of different criteria.

Bibliography

1. Statista. (2018). Total online retail sales revenue in China from 2014 to 2017* (in trillion yuan). Retrieved December 2, 2017, from https://www.statista.com/ statistics/655849/china-total-retail-sales-online-revenue/

2. South China Morning Post. (2016). Urban legend: China's tiered city system explained. Retrieved December 2, 2017, from http://multimedia.scmp.com/2016/ cities/

3. 中国电子商务研究中心 (November 14, 2016). 2016年中国消费者网络消费洞察报告与网购指南. Retrieved December 15, 2017, from http://www.100ec.cn/zt/16zgxfz/

4. Bain & Company. (June 29, 2017). China's Two-Speed Growth: In and Out of the Home. China Shopper Report 2017, Retrieved from http://www.bain.com/ publications/articles/china-shopper-report-2017-chinas-two-speed-growth-in-and-out-of-the-home.aspx

5. McKinsey & Company. (March 2012). Meet the Chinese consumer of 2020. Retrieved November 28, 2017, from https://www.mckinsey.com/global-themes/asia-pacific/ meet-the-chinese-consumer-of-2020

6. AccentureStrategy. (n.d.). Digital Disconnect in Customer Engagement. Retrieved December 15, 2017, from https://www.accenture.com/us-en/insight-digital-disconnect-customer-engagement

7. China National Tourism Administration. (July 31, 2017). 砥砺奋进的五年:我国国际旅游持续保持顺差. Retrieved December 16, 2017, from http://www.cnta.gov.cn/zwgk/ lysj/201707/t20170730_833612.shtml

8. Central Intelligence Agency Library. (2017). The World FactBook. Retrieved December 16, 2017, from https://www.cia.gov/library/publications/the-world-factbook/fields/2102.html

9. China's National Bureau of Statistics. (2011). 中国统计年鉴. Retrieved December 16, 2017, from http://www.stats.gov.cn/tjsj/ndsj/2011/indexeh.htm

10. Central Intelligence Agency Library. (2017). The World FactBook. Retrieved December 16, 2017, from https://www.cia.gov/library/publications/the-world-factbook/fields/2054.html#xx

11.   Washington University in St.Louis. (January 25, 2017). Global experts convene in China to tackle challenges of aging population. Retrieved December 21, 2017, from https://source.wustl.edu/2017/01/global-experts-convene-china-tackle-challenges-aging-population/

12.   China National Tourism Administration. (July 6, 2017). 旅游需求增长迅速 "银发游"市场：潜力大 待深耕. Retrieved December 21, 2017, from http://cnta.gov.cn/xxfb/hydt/201607/t20160705_776285.shtml

13.   UIS.Stat. (January 28, 2018). Education(full dataset). Retrieved January 29, 2018, from http://data.uis.unesco.org/Index.aspx?DataSetCode=EDULIT_DS#

14.   South China Morning Post. (August 10, 2017). There are 200 million of them and they're richer than ever. So why aren't China's singles doing more for the economy?. Retrieved December 21, 2017, from http://www.scmp.com/business/china-business/article/2106279/theres-200-million-them-and-theyre-richer-ever-so-why-arent

15.   Ali Research. (May 23, 2017). 中国消费新趋势:三大动力塑造中国消费新客群. Retrieved December 22, 2017, from http://i.aliresearch.com/img/20170523/20170523171542.pdf

16.   京东研究院. (November 19, 2017). 2017女性消费报告. Retrieved December 22, 2017, from http://www.useit.com.cn/thread-17174-1-1.html

17.   China's National Bureau of Statistics. (July 18, 2017). 孟庆欣：上半年消费品市场稳健发展. Retrieved December 22, 2017, from http://www.stats.gov.cn/tjsj/sjjd/201707/t20170718_1514078.html

18.   Deloitte (2016). China E-Retail Market Report 2016. Retrieved December 23, 2017, from https://www2.deloitte.com/content/dam/Deloitte/cn/Documents/cip/deloitte-cn-cip-china-online-retail-market-report-en-170123.pdf

19.   China Internet Watch. (November 29, 2017). Guangdong leads China's online retail market with over 23%. Retrieved December 23, 2017, from https://www.chinainternetwatch.com/ 22710/guangdong-online-retail-2016/

20.   PricewaterhouseCoopers. (2017) eCommerce in China - the future is already here. Retrieved December 23, 2017, from https://www.pwccn.com/en/industries/retail-and-consumer/publications/total-retail-survey-2017-china-cut.html

21.   Credit Suisse. (October 13, 2017). The Chinese Consumer in 2017: The Lifestyle Upgrade. Retrieved December 23, 2017, from https://www.credit-suisse.com/corporate/en/articles/news-and-expertise/the-chinese-consumer-in-2017-the-lifestyle-upgrade-201710.html

22. China National Tourism Administration. (November 8, 2017). 2016年中国旅游业统计公报. Retrieved December 23, 2017, from http://www.cnta.gov.cn/zwgk/lysj/201711/t20171108_846343.shtml

23. Wikipedia. (n.d.). 2008 Chinese milk scandal. Retrieved December 27, 2017, from https://en.wikipedia.org/wiki/2008_Chinese_milk_scandal

24. Chatterbox (November 9, 2017). The 2017 WeChat Data Report. Retrieved December 27, 2017, from http://blog.wechat.com/2017/11/09/the-2017-wechat-data-report/

25. McKinsey & Company. (August 2017). Chinese luxury consumers: More global, more demanding, still spending. Retrieved December 27, 2017, from https://www.mckinsey.com/business-functions/marketing-and-sales/our-insights/chinese-luxury-consumers-more-global-more-demanding-still-spending

26. Bain & Company. (October 25, 2017). Global personal luxury goods market returns to healthy growth, reaching a fresh high of €262 billion in 2017. Retrieved December 27, 2017, from http://www.bain.com/about/press/press-releases/press-release-2017-global-fall-luxury-market-study.aspx

27. Rambourg, E. (2014). The Bling Dynasty: Why the Reign of Chinese Luxury Shoppers Has Only just Begun. John Wiley & Sons.

28. iResearch (October 9, 2016). 2016年中国视频网站付费用户典型案例研究报告——乐视影视会员洞察研究报告. Retrieved December 27, 2017, from http://www.iresearch.com.cn/report/2653.html

29. GfK Global. (November 19, 2016). New Potential for the Imaging Market. Retrieved January 1, 2018, from http://www.gfk.com/zh/insights/press-release/new-potential-for-the-imaging-market-1/

30. Accenture Strategy. (February 22, 2017). 埃森哲战略：五大新秘诀，提升中国消费者忠诚度. Retrieved January 5, 2018, from https://www.accenture.com/cn-zh/company-consumer-loyalty-improvement

31. Consulate-General of the Kingdom of the Netherlands in Shanghai. (January 2017). China Cross-Border E-Commerce. Retrieved January 6, 2018, from https://www.rvo.nl/sites/default/files/2017/03/Cross-Border%20E-Commere%20Guidebook%20FINAL%20FINAL.PDF

32. Deloitte, China E-Retail Market Report 2016. (See endnote 18)

33. LinkedIn Learning. (January 24, 2017). Digital in 2017 Global Overview. Retrieved January 7, 2018, from https://www.slideshare.net/wearesocialsg/digital-in-2017-global-overview

34.   36kr. (September 29, 2017). 36氪专访 | 日播放量破十亿的抖音，要如何
      撬开商业化的大门？. Retrieved January 7, 2018, from http://www.sohu.
      com/a/195438403_114778

35.   ChinaDaily. (November 11, 2017). Toutiao buying Musical.ly for $1b. Retrieved
      January 7, 2018, from http://www.chinadaily.com.cn/business/tech/2017-11/11/
      content_34392625.htm

36.   快手(n.d.). 关于快手. Retrieved January 7, 2018, from https://www.kuaishou.com/
      about.html

37.   洪兴会. (April 25, 2017). 喜马拉雅，如何将一款APP做到3亿用户（上）. Retrieved
      January 7, 2018, from http://www.sohu.com/a/136367812_575369

38.   Linkedin. (n.d.). Xiaohongshu. Retrieved January 7, 2018, from https://www.linkedin.
      com/company/10269563/

39.   China Internet Watch. (November 9, 2017). WeChat Statistics Report Q3 2017;
      MAU reached 980 million. Retrieved January 7, 2018, from https://www.
      chinainternetwatch.com/22822/wechat-data-report-2017/

40.   Quartz. (May 03, 2017). China's Tencent is a sleeping giant in the global artificial
      intelligence race. Retrieved January 7, 2018, from https://qz.com/974408/tencents-
      wechat-gives-it-an-advantage-in-the-global-artificial-intelligence-race/

41.   South China Morning Post (April 25, 2017). WeChat is top workplace communications
      app for 90 per cent of Chinese professionals. Retrieved January 15, 2018, from
      http://www.scmp.com/tech/apps-gaming/article/2090472/wechat-top-workplace-
      communications-app-90-cent-chinese

42.   Technode. (November 10, 2017). WeChat becomes "a lifestyle" as senior users,
      calls, and payments all see large increases. Retrieved January 15, 2018, from https://
      technode.com/2017/11/10/wechat-becomes-a-lifestyle-as-senior-users-calls-and-
      payments-all-see-large-increases/

43.   Reuters. (February 4, 2017). WeChat users send 46 billion digital red packets over
      Lunar New Year - Xinhua. Retrieved January 18, 2018, from https://www.reuters.com/
      article/us-lunar-newyear-wechat-redpackets/wechat-users-send-46-billion-digital-
      red-packets-over-lunar-new-year-xinhua-idUSKBN15J0BG

44.   Hollander, R. (Jan. 23, 2018). WeChat touts success of its 580,000 'mini programs'.
      Retrieved January 29, 2018, from http://www.businessinsider.com/wechat-touts-
      success-of-its-580000-mini-programs-2018-1

45.   WeChat Pay. (n.d.). Cross-border Payment. Retrieved January 29, 2018, from https://
      pay.weixin.qq.com/wechatpay_guide/intro_settle.shtml

46. Weibo Corporation. (November 7, 2017). Weibo Reports Third Quarter 2017 Financial Results. Retrieved January 20, 2018, from http://ir.weibo.com/phoenix. zhtml?c=253076&p=irol-newsArticle&ID=2314816

47. Chen, F. (July 24, 2014). Has Tencent lost the Weibo war to Sina?. Retrieved January 22, 2018, from http://www.ejinsight.com/20140724-tencent-weibo-sina-weibo/

48. Hatton, C. (February 24, 2015). Is Weibo on the way out?. Retrieved January 22, 2018, from http://www.bbc.com/news/blogs-china-blog-31598865

49. Dannieli (October 19, 2016). Behind the rebirth of Weibo, Twitter take note. Retrieved January 22, 2018, from https://www.chinatechinsights.com/analysis/2147554.html

50. Cao, B. (February 29, 2012). Sina's Weibo Outlook Buoys Internet Stock Gains: China Overnight. Retrieved January 22, 2018, from https://www.bloomberg.com/news/articles/2012-02-28/sina-s-weibo-outlook-buoys-internet-stock-gains-in-n-y-china-overnight

51. Xu, C. (August 1, 2016). A Field Guide to China's Most Indispensible Meme. Retrieved January 22, 2018, from https://motherboard.vice.com/en_us/article/bmvd74/china-meme-face-a-biaoqing-field-guide

52. Jing Daily. (June 14, 2017). How These 10 New KOL 'Rules' on Weibo Could Affect Luxury Brands in China. Retrieved January 24, 2018, from https://jingdaily.com/10-new-kols-rules-weibo-luxury-brands/

53. 新浪综合. (March 23, 2017). 微博网红电商平台上线 加速网红经济普及. Retrieved January 24, 2018, from http://tech.sina.com.cn/i/2017-03-23/doc-ifycstww0805356.shtml

54. Zhong, I. (June 8, 2017). Alibaba Analyst Meeting Day One: Targets 45% – 49% Revenue Growth, Renames Key Metrics. Retrieved January 29, 2018, from https://www.barrons.com/articles/alibaba-investor-day-targets-45-49-revenue-growth-renames-key-metrics-1496915095

55. Zennon Kapron & Michelle Meertens (April 2017). Better Than Cash Alliance China Report April 2017 (1). Retrieved January 29, 2018, from https://www.scribd.com/document/346080647/better-than-cash-alliance-china-report-april-2017-1

56. Hatton, C. (October 26, 2015). China 'social credit': Beijing sets up huge system. Retrieved January 29, 2018, from http://www.bbc.com/news/world-asia-china-34592186

57. South China Morning Post. (December 26, 2017). WeChat poised to become China's official electronic ID system. Retrieved January 29, 2018, from http://www.scmp.com/tech/social-gadgets/article/2125736/wechat-poised-become-chinas-official-electronic-id-system

58. 36kr. (2018). 腾讯云：从"互联网+"到"智能+"，从连接人到连接各行各业. Retrieved January 29, 2018, from https://36kr.com/p/5102282.html

59. 中新经纬. (2018). 都做新零售，阿里腾讯京东有何不同？. Retrieved January 29, 2018, from http://www.sohu.com/a/203797636_561670

60. Tencent Technology. (2018). 京东、腾讯联合宣布推出无界零售解决方案_科技_腾讯网. Retrieved January 29, 2018, from http://tech.qq.com/a/20171017/032785.htm

61. Alizila. (2018). A Dose of New Retail for China's Convenience Stores, Retrieved March, 2018, from http://www.alizila.com/alibaba-gives-dose-new-retail-china-convenience-stores/

62. The Independent. (2018). A company you've never heard of just eclipsed Facebook last week. Retrieved March, 28, 2018, from https://www.independent.co.uk/life-style/gadgets-and-tech/tencent-facebook-china-wechat-revenue-500-billion-alibaba-honour-of-kings-a8076861.html

63. Econsultancy. (2018) JD.com: More Than Ecommerce. Retrieved March, 19, 2018, from https://www.econsultancy.com/reports/jd-com-more-than-ecommerce

64. China Internet Watch. (2018). China B2C online retail market overview 2017, led by Tmall and JD. Retrieved March, 28, 2018, from https://www.chinainternetwatch.com/23369/retail-b2c-q4-2017/#ixzz59sWeXJedhttps://www.chinainternetwatch.com/23369/retail-b2c-q4-2017/#ixzz59sWeXJed

65. TechCrunch. (2018) Tencent and JD.com invest $863M into e-commerce firm Vipshop to battle Alibaba. Retrieved March, 28, 2018, from https://techcrunch.com/2017/12/17/tencent-jd-vipshop-863-million/

66. Asean Today. (2017). Alipay and Tenpay compete head-to-head for overseas market share. Retrieved February, 4, 2018, from https://www.aseantoday.com/2017/09/alipay-and-tenpay-compete-head-to-head-for-overseas-market-share/

67. Wired. (2017). Big data meets Big Brother as China moves to rate its citizens. Retrieved March, 20, 2018, from http://www.wired.co.uk/article/chinese-government-social-credit-score-privacy-invasion

68. The Financial Times. (2018). China changes tack on 'social credit' scheme plan. Retrieved March, 20, 2018, from https://www.ft.com/content/f772a9ce-60c4-11e7-91a7-502f7ee26895

69. Sohu. (2017). 阿里、腾讯发力征信体系，中国离信用社会还远吗？ Retrieved March, 21, 2018, from http://www.sohu.com/a/164997205_353364

70. The Economist. (2017). Shenzhen is a hothouse of innovation. Retrieved March, 28, 2018, from https://www.economist.com/news/special-report/21720076-copycats-are-out-innovators-are-shenzhen-hothouse-innovation

71. South China Morning Post. (2018). Shenzhen Superstars is a primer on China's rival to Silicon Valley from the pen of an unconventional Swede. Retrieved March, 28, 2018, from http://www.scmp.com/magazines/post-magazine/books/article/2130592/shenzhen-side-story-amazing-chinese-city-seen-through

72. South China Morning Post. (2017). Lenovo hangs on to No 2 spot as global PC sales beat forecast. Retrieved January, 29, 2018, from http://www.scmp.com/tech/leaders-founders/article/2114813/lenovo-holds-worlds-no-2-pc-supplier-amid-signs-market

73. The Verge. (2017). Huawei has surpassed Apple as the world's second largest smartphone brand. Retrieved October, 13, 2017, from https://www.theverge.com/2017/9/6/16259810/huawei-apple-global-smartphone-sales

74. CNN. (2018). Alibaba bets on Olympics to make it a household name. Retrieved February, 29, 2018, from http://money.cnn.com/2018/02/20/news/companies/alibaba-olympics-brand/index.html

75. Asia Times. (2017). Guangzhou-Shenzhen tech corridor takes aim at Silicon Valley. Retrieved January, 3, 2018, from http://www.atimes.com/article/guangzhou-shenzhen-tech-corridor-takes-aim-silicon-valley/

76. Forbes. (2017). Beijing -- Not Silicon Valley -- Is The World's Top Tech Hub, Report Says. Retrieved March, 12, 2018 from https://www.forbes.com/sites/chynes/2017/11/02/has-beijing-unseated-silicon-valley-as-the-worlds-top-tech-hub-one-report-says-yes/#3b3de9df7acf

77. South China Morning Post. (2017). Supercomputer superpower China takes biggest lead over US in 25 years. Retrieved March, 29, 2018, from http://www.scmp.com/news/china/policies-politics/article/2119906/supercomputer-superpower-china-takes-biggest-lead-over

78. eMarketer. (2018). Blockchain Finds Broader Applications in China. Retrieved March, 29, 2018, from https://www.emarketer.com/content/blockchain-finds-broader-applications-in-china

79. Coindesk. (2018). China's Biggest Political Event Sees Blockchain Praise. Retrieved March, 13, 2018, from https://www.coindesk.com/chinas-biggest-political-event-sees-talk-of-blockchains-potential/

80. Science. (2018). China's massive investment in artificial intelligence has an insidious downside. Retrieved February, 28, 2018, from http://www.sciencemag.org/news/2018/02/china-s-massive-investment-artificial-intelligence-has-insidious-downside

81. Machine Design. (2018). China's Plan to Become a Robotic Powerhouse. Retrieved February, 23, 2018, from http://www.machinedesign.com/motion-control/china-s-plan-become-robotic-powerhouse

82. CNBC. (2017). China's blueprint to crush the US robotics industry. Retrieved March, 29, 2018, from https://www.cnbc.com/2017/09/06/chinas-blueprint-to-crush-the-us-robotics-industry.html

83. The Telegraph. (2017). China's tech companies leading the way with robotics. Retrieved January, 9, 2018, from https://www.telegraph.co.uk/news/world/china-watch/technology/china-tech-companies-aiming-smarten-world-robots/

84. Business Insider. (2017). Here are the world's largest drone companies and manufacturers to watch and invest in. Retrieved 20 March, 12, 2018, from http://www.businessinsider.com/top-drone-manufacturers-companies-invest-stocks-2017-07

85. Drone life. (2017). DJI Wins 2017 Emmy for Technology and Engineering. Retrieved February, 5, 2018, from https://dronelife.com/2017/08/31/dji-wins-2017-emmy-technology-engineering/

86. KPMG. (2017). The Fintech100 – Announcing the world's leading fintech innovators for 2017. Retrieved March, 14, 2017, from https://home.kpmg.com/xx/en/home/media/press-releases/2017/11/the-fintech-100-announcing-the-worlds-leading-fintech-innovators-for-2017.html

87. eMarketer. (2017). Five Insights into China's Virtual Reality Sector. Retrieved 14 February 2018, from https://www.emarketer.com/Article/Five-Insights-Chinas-Virtual-Reality-Sector/1016179

88. TechNode. (2017). This Chinese film studio is showing the potential of VR content · Retrieved March, 10, 2018, from https://technode.com/2017/08/14/this-chinese-film-studio-is-showing-the-potential-of-vr-content/

89. South China Morning Post. (2015) 'Super puppies' created in DNA manipulation: Chinese mainland scientists turn genetic editing into reality. Retrieved February, 8, 2018, from http://www.scmp.com/tech/science-research/article/1870058/super-puppies-created-dna-manipulation-chinese-mainland

90. CNN (2017). Chinese firm clones gene-edited dog in bid to treat cardiovascular disease. Retrieved March, 29, 2018, from https://edition.cnn.com/2017/12/25/health/china-dog-cloning-for-disease-intl/index.html

91. Wikipedia. (2018) Solar power in China. Retrieved March, 29, 2018, from https://en.wikipedia.org/wiki/Solar_power_in_China

92. South China Morning Post. (2017) China already the clear powerhouse in electric cars. Retrieved March, 16, 2018, from http://www.scmp.com/business/companies/article/2126083/china-already-clear-powerhouse-electric-cars

93. Time. (2018). Why China Will Beat Tesla in the Electric Car Race. Retrieved March, 6, 2018, from http://time.com/5107488/why-china-will-beat-tesla-electric-car-race/

94. Space.com. (2013) China Lands On The Moon: Historic Robotic Lunar Landing Includes 1st Chinese Rover. Retrieved March, 22, 2018, from https://www.space.com/23968-china-moon-rover-historic-lunar-landing.html

95. Live Science. (2018). Chinese Scientists Unveil Plans for Weird Hypersonic Jet with Extra Wing. Retrieved 26 February 2018, from https://www.livescience.com/61849-china-designs-hypersonic-plane.html

96. Youtube. JD.com (2017). Augmented Reality and Virtual Reality for e-Commerce. Retrieved March, 12, 2018, from https://www.youtube.com/watch?v=5ru2oJgekN4

97. Forbes. (2017). VR/AR in China: An Emerging Giant?. Retrieved March, 14, 2018, from https://www.forbes.com/sites/charliefink/2017/12/19/vrar-in-china-an-emerging-giant/#ed40e1675738

98. Forbes. (2016). China's Year Of Virtual Reality. Retrieved March, 22, 2018, from https://www.forbes.com/sites/lisachanson/2016/12/23/chinas-year-of-virtual-reality/

99. Forbes. (2017). Would You Buy A Car Online? Why Chinese Motorists Are Skipping The Dealership For Virtual Showrooms. Retrieved February, 18, 2018, from https://www.forbes.com/sites/ywang/2017/12/12/would-you-buy-a-car-online-why-chinese-motorists-are-skipping-the-dealership-for-virtual-showrooms/#786e42d83132

100. South China Morning Post. (2017). Huawei, Xiaomi lead Chinese brands' stranglehold on world's largest smartphone market. Retrieved March, 22, 2018, from http://www.scmp.com/tech/article/2118660/huawei-xiaomi-lead-chinese-brands-stranglehold-worlds-largest-smartphone-market

101. The Wall Street Journal (2018). Who's Afraid of Huawei? Security Worries Spread Beyond the U.S.. Retrieved March, 12, 2018, from https://www.wsj.com/articles/whos-afraid-of-huawei-security-worries-spread-beyond-the-u-s-1521561391

102. South China Morning Post. (2018). China's Huawei says rivals using politics to keep it out of US for fear of competition. Retrieved March, 23, 2018, from http://www.scmp.com/tech/social-gadgets/article/2134669/chinas-huawei-says-rivals-using-politics-keep-it-out-us-fear

103. Bloomberg. (2018). Huawei Is in Talks to Build a Blockchain-Ready Smartphone. Retrieved March, 29, 2018, from https://www.bloomberg.com/news/articles/2018-03-21/huawei-said-to-be-in-talks-to-build-blockchain-ready-smartphone

104. The Hindu Business Line. (2017). Haier tops euromonitor's major appliances global brand rankings for 8th consecutive year. Retrieved March, 12, 2018, from https://www.thehindubusinessline.com/business-wire/haier-tops-euromonitors-major-appliances-global-brand-rankings-for-8th-consecutive-year/article9524357.ece

105. South China Morning Post. (2017). Haier bought GE Appliances for US$5.6 billion. Now it's working on fixing it. Retrieved March, 14, 2018, from http://www.scmp.com/business/companies/article/2116486/chinas-haier-has-plan-help-continue-turnaround-ge-appliances

106. South China Morning Post. (2015). Chinese electronics giant Haier to open 1 million WeChat stores by 2016 as firm targets e-commerce. Retrieved March, 16, 2018, from http://www.scmp.com/tech/enterprises/article/1852649/haier-open-1m-wechat-stores-2016-electronics-giant-targets-e

107. Strategy+Business (2018). Why Haier Is Reorganizing Itself around the Internet of Things. Retrieved March, 8, 2018, from https://www.strategy-business.com/article/Why-Haier-Is-Reorganizing-Itself-around-the-Internet-of-Things?gko=895fe

108. Recode. (2017). DJI is running away with the drone market. Retrieved February, 19, 2018, from https://www.recode.net/2017/4/14/14690576/drone-market-share-growth-charts-dji-forecast

109. South China Morning Post. (2017). Geely buys into Swedish truck maker AB Volvo to reinforce globalisation drive. Retrieved March, 10, 2018, from http://www.scmp.com/business/companies/article/2125872/geely-buys-swedish-truck-maker-ab-volvo-reinforce-globalisation

110. Reuters. (2013) China's Geely buys black cab maker Manganese Bronze. Retrieved March, 14, 2018, from https://uk.reuters.com/article/uk-manganesebronze/chinas-geely-buys-black-cab-maker-manganese-bronze-idUKBRE9100BW20130201

111. Reuters. (2017). Chinese-owned Club Med to open 15 new resorts by 2019. Retrieved March, 12, 2018, from https://www.reuters.com/article/us-clubmed-expansion/chinese-owned-club-med-to-open-15-new-resorts-by-2019-idUSKBN15A271

112. The Financial Times. (2017) AC Milan sold to Rossoneri Sport Investment Lux. Retrieved March, 16, 2018, from https://www.ft.com/content/656dfd32-61f1-3d95-a26e-43ef231eb9d0

113. South China Morning Post. (2017) Chinese owner to be involved in Grindr's operations after deal. Retrieved March, 5, 2018, from http://www.scmp.com/business/companies/article/2095674/chinese-tech-firm-fully-buy-gay-dating-app-grindr

114. PetaPixel. (2018). 500px Acquired by VCG, the Getty Images of China. Retrieved March, 7, 2018, from https://petapixel.com/2018/02/26/500px-acquired-vcg-getty-images-china/

115. CNN (2012). China firm buys AMC to form world's largest cinema chain Retrieved March, 22, 2018, from https://edition.cnn.com/2012/05/21/business/china-amc-wanda-theater/

116. Deadline Hollywood (2016). Is 'Warcraft's Outsized China Box Office A Game-Changer For Hollywood?. Retrieved March, 14, 2018, from http://deadline.com/2016/06/warcraft-box-office-analysis-china-future-1201772400/

117. PR Newswire. (2017). Mobike, AT&T and Qualcomm Collaborate on Mobile IoT Smart Bike Share Technology. Retrieved March, 10, 2018, from https://www.prnewswire.com/news-releases/mobike-att-and-qualcomm-collaborate-on-mobile-iot-smart-bike-share-technology-300516548.html

118. The Street. (2017). Alibaba's Jack Ma: 'By 2035, We Will Be the Fifth Largest Economy in the World'. Retrieved March, 12, 2018, from https://www.thestreet.com/story/14188256/1/alibaba-s-jack-ma-by-2035-we-will-be-the-fifth-largest-economy-in-the-world.html

About the Author

Ashley is an entrepreneur, speaker, author, vlogger and podcaster. Her trademark expression is "Let's go get them," and she does. She's fluent in Mandarin, Russian, German and English. As a marketer and social media agency head with more than ten years of professional experience in the region, she has seen the transformation of China's online world firsthand. Her specialties are China market entry, Chinese consumers and social media.

Ashley is the founder of multiple startups, including social media marketing agency Alarice (alarice.com.hk) and training platform ChoZan (chozan.co). Through Alarice, she and her team help clients from overseas make a splash on Chinese social media as well as help Chinese brands conquer Western social media. This runs the gamut from social media strategy, account set up and content creation to community management. Through ChoZan, which specializes in social media education and training, Ashley does corporate training workshops, speaking engagements and guest lectures.

She has appeared in Forbes, CNBC, Huffington Post, the SCMP and has been a speaker at the China Marketing Summit, WeChat Conference, TEDx and more.

If you need a speaker or trainer for social media marketing, contact Ashley's team at ashley@chozan.co. Learn more at ashleytalks.com.

You can also follow Ashley on:
LinkedIn.com/in/AshleyGalina/	YouTube.com/c/AshleyTalksChina
Instagram.com/Ashley.Lina/	Facebook.com/AshleyTalksChina
Podcast https://apple.co/2FK7tRF	Twitter.com/AshleyDudarenok

Copyright © 2018 Alarice International

All rights reserved. This book or any portion thereof may not be reproduced or used in any manner whatsoever without the express written permission of the publisher except for the use of brief quotations in the press or book reviews.

First Printing, 2018
ISBN 978-0-692-06693-5
2102, luki Tower,
5 O'Brien Road,
Wan Chai,
Hong Kong

Although the author and publisher have made every effort to ensure that the information in this book was correct at press time, they do not assume and hereby disclaim any liability to any party for any loss, damage, or disruption caused by errors or omissions, whether such errors or omissions result from negligence, accident, or any other cause.

The publisher has made every effort to ensure that URLs for external websites referred to in this book are correct and active at the time of going to press. However, the publisher has no responsibility for the websites and can make no guarantee that a site will remain live or that the content is or will remain appropriate.

Every effort has been made to trace all copyright holders but if any have been inadvertently overlooked the publisher will be pleased to include any necessary credits in any subsequent reprint or edition.